50 CONTEMPORARY FASHION DESIGNERS
YOU SHOULD KNOW

50 CONTEMPORARY FASHION DESIGNERS

YOU SHOULD KNOW

Doria Santlofer

Prestel

Munich · London · New York

Front cover: Alice Temperley London Fall/Winter 2012/13 campaign
Frontispiece: Riccardo Tisci for Givenchy Fall/Winter 2008/09 collection, Paris Fashion Week
Pages 10–11: Mandy Coon Fall/Winter 2012/13 collection

Prestel Verlag, Munich
A member of Verlagsgruppe Random House GmbH

Prestel Verlag
Neumarkter Strasse 28
81673 Munich
Tel. +49 (0)89 4136-0
Fax +49 (0)89 4136-2335

www.prestel.de

Prestel Publishing Ltd.
4 Bloomsbury Place
London WC1A 2QA
Tel. +44 (0)20 7323-5004
Fax +44 (0)20 7636-8004

Prestel Publishing
900 Broadway, Suite 603
New York, NY 10003
Tel. +1 (212) 995-2720
Fax +1 (212) 995-2733

www.prestel.com

Library of Congress Control Number is available; British Library Cataloguing-in-Publication Data: a catalogue record for this book is available from the British Library; Deutsche Nationalbibliothek holds a record of this publication in the Deutsche Nationalbibliografie; detailed bibliographical data can be found under: http://dnb.d-nb.de

Prestel books are available worldwide. Please contact your nearest bookseller or one of the above addresses for information concerning your local distributor.

Project management by Claudia Stäuble
Assistance by Franziska Stegmann
Copyedited by Jonathan Fox, Barcelona
Picture research by Janina Baur
Production by Nele Krüger and zwischenschritt, Rainald Schwarz, Munich
Cover and Design by LIQUID, Agentur für Gestaltung, Augsburg
Layout by zwischenschritt, Rainald Schwarz, Munich
Origination by ReproLine Mediateam
Printed and bound by Druckerei Uhl GmbH & Co. KG, Radolfzell

Verlagsgruppe Random House FSC®-DEU-0100
The FSC®-certified paper Hello Fat Matt has been
produced by mill Condat, Le Lardin Saint-Lazare, France.

Printed in Germany

ISBN 978-3-7913-4713-4

CONTENTS

1940 The first McDonald's restaurant opens

1961 Construction of the Berlin Wall

1969 Woodstock Festival

1930   1935   1940   1945   1950   1955   1960   1965   1970   1975   1980

Haider Ackermann Spring/Summer 2010 Prêt-à-
Porter show, Paris Fashion Week

1993 Bill Clinton sworn in as 42nd US president

2007 The Apple iPhone goes on sale

2016 Olympic Games in Rio de Janeiro

1981 First recognized cases of AIDS

2001 First same-sex marriage in the Netherlands

2011 After 14 years of collaboration, Dior suspends John Galliano

1985   1990   1995   2000   2005   2010   2015   2020   2025   2030   2035

HAIDER ACKERMANN

The avant-garde aesthetic comes naturally to Haider Ackermann, the Colombian designer who has become known for his fluid draping and sophisticated sense of color. In 2010, the Belgian-trained designer presented a stellar and evocative collection and catapulted himself into fashion-world stardom.

Born in Santa Fe de Bogota, Columbia in 1971, Ackermann's cartographer father moved the family around several times throughout his childhood, bringing them on travels throughout Europe and Africa. Upon graduating from high school in the Netherlands, Ackermann moved to Belgium in his early twenties to study at the Royal Academy of Antwerp. In 2001, after interning for John Galliano, the young designer launched his own womenswear label, presenting his first collection in Paris for Fall 2002. Ackermann's Belgian training is perhaps the reason for the designer's darker, more austere sensibility, albeit one that never fails to be beautiful. Now, a decade after his debut, Ackermann's draped and tailored style has made an immense impact on fashion.

In November 2010, after seasons of solid reviews yet quieter commercial success, great praise from Karl Lagerfeld was bestowed upon the Colombian-born designer. When asked who would be the person to replace Lagerfeld at Chanel, the famed designer replied: "At the moment I'd say Haider Ackermann." So, when Ackermann presented his Fall 2011 collection the following spring, all eyes were on him as possible heir to the Chanel throne. And Haider Ackermann did not disappoint. In a show that critics hailed as "transporting" and "exuberant," the designer maintained many of his signature elements, including draping on beautifully wrapped coats, a long, lean silhouette, and small, cinched waists. The show opened with a series of black coats, belted at the waist and trailing in back. As it progressed, the palette turned to rich jewel tones of deep burgundy, intense teal, and cobalt blue. The jackets, which were wrapped and twisted with an expert skill, came in silk, leather, and suede, worn over slim-fitting slouchy pants and wide-leg, more masculine-inspired trousers. While the clothes were more masculine on the whole, the collection was not without elements of sex appeal, like the asymmetric body-conscious skirt with cutaways at the thighs or the draped silk tops that opened under jackets to reveal slivers of skin. So beautiful and romantic was Ackermann's Fall 2011 collection that many, it was said, were moved to tears.

The following year marked another triumphant season for the designer. The Fall 2012 collection focused on organic shapes and a deeper exploration into color. The show opened with a fitted, cropped jacket in sage green, firmly belted at the waist with a wide brown leather belt and paired with a form fitting black skirt. Despite the sleek intro, signature Ackermann shapes were not far behind. "I can't help myself," said the designer of his trademark. "I love to wrap." The wrapped jackets featured structured peplums, while several of the dresses were draped from a point at the middle of the chest, creating a shape that resembled a butterfly. A wrapped leather bomber, tightly belted, was worn over skinny metallic pants, and coats with full collars were shown with high-waisted trousers. The color pairings were a triumph in and of themselves, with deep aubergine mixed with warm marigold and a rich cobalt blue layered over maroon, gray, and rust.

In the past two years the fashion world at large has taken note of Haider Ackermann, a designer once celebrated by a much smaller, yet devoted, circle of followers. Now, his elongated silhouettes and sculptural drapes have attracted a whole new audience and a welcome group of customers. His impeccable tailoring and romantic aesthetic are sexy without being obvious and dramatic without being over-the-top. It's this fastidious craftsmanship, and the fact that his runway shows have the ability to invoke tears, that has made Haider Ackermann one of this decade's most relevant designers.

1971 Born in Colombia
1994 Enrolls at Antwerp Fashion Academy of Fine Arts; interns for John Galliano
2001 Launches own womenswear label; first collection presented in Paris in March
2003 Directs collections for Ruffo Research
2004 Wins Swiss Textiles Award
2005 Contributes to *A Magazine* as guest curator
2010 Presents capsule collection for both men and women as guest designer at Pitti W in Florence
2011 Karl Lagerfeld refers to him as his ideal successor

Haider Ackermann, 2010

1945 Marilyn Monroe discovered
as a photo model

1959 First Barbie doll shown at
a toy fair in New York

1978 Forming of
the band
Duran Duran

1930   1935   1940   1945   1950   1955   1960   1965   1970   1975   1980

Steven Alan Fall 2012 presentation,
Mercedes-Benz Fashion Week, New York

1981 Ronald Reagan sworn in as 40th US president

1999 First e-book reader

1996 First cloned mammal (Dolly the Sheep)

2012 Picasso's *Nu au Plateau de Sculpteur* fetches $106.5 million at Christie's

2000 Tate Modern Gallery opens in London

1985 · 1990 · 1995 · 2000 · 2005 · 2010 · 2015 · 2020 · 2025 · 2030 · 2035

STEVEN ALAN

With eleven stores located across the United States, Steven Alan and his signature label, Steven Alan Collection, has become the go-to brand for updated American classics.

The man behind the brand, born Steven Alan Grossman, grew up in New York, studied art in high school, and had a passionate interest in design. In 1994, he opened his first store, a small women's multi-brand boutique that focused on accessories. Two years later, Alan began representing some of the emerging designers he carried, launching the Steven Alan Showroom, and gained a reputation among a young, downtown set of customers who deemed him a talented curator and tastemaker. In 1999, with his position as a notable retailer, coupled with his own style aesthetic, Alan started making his first pieces of clothing and he began with a classic: the men's button-down shirt, to which he applied subtle details and a particular washing process that resulted in a shirt with perfect fit that looked as though it had been worn for years and just the right amount of slouch and softness. Now known as the Reverse Seam Shirt, this early model has become a Steven Alan signature, featuring a slightly tailored body, French seams at the side, and a twisted placket.

Soon the idea of the perfect shirt expanded to include a line of boyfriend-inspired women's shirts. The concept and details were the same, applying Alan's classic shape to women. From there, both collections grew and grew, each starting from the signature shirt and expanding into full ready-to-wear lines. The collection, said Alan, is about the wardrobe "essentials for life in the big city." As a native New Yorker, it is something he understands well, and his customers agree, stocking up on pieces at one of the several New York stores located in Tribeca, Nolita, the West Village, the Upper West Side, and Brooklyn. The expansion didn't stop there. Within a decade of launching, Alan had added a store in East Hampton along with three stores in and around Los Angeles and one in San Francisco. The showroom has also been steadily growing, with Alan representing an eclectic group of young talent. Now, with over twenty designers on his roster, Steven Alan has created a mini fashion empire with

a highly curated aesthetic that can be described as "classic American with a twist."

For Spring 2011, Steven Alan staged his first formal presentation, showcasing, on models, both his men's and women's collections along with his accessories. The inspiration for spring was travel, specifically the Mediterranean. The look was based on the idea of "getting out of New York, but having the New York sensibilities in a different place," said the designer. For women, Alan showed summery trousers in cotton and linen along with casual, pleated minidresses and breezy, printed jumpsuits. The men's collection featured several variations on Alan's now-famous shirting as well as vests, jackets, and some casual, slim-fitting, cinched-waist pants. The citified beach look was the epitome of relaxed sophistication.

For his Fall 2012 collection, Alan drew his inspiration from the Diego Rivera exhibition at the Metropolitan Museum of Art, taking elements of ideas in Rivera's paintings and distilling them into pieces that made sense for his brand. Rivera's Mexican heritage came across in the striped jackets and jersey dresses, as well as the knits that had been handmade in South America. On the whole, Alan's collection was muted, his palette a mix of primarily grays and sepias, with occasional pops of bright red and a darker burgundy. The menswear line incorporated dressier elements, such as tailored suiting in washed wool and herringbone tweed. The womenswear, as well, came in masculine tweeds and checks, with the more feminine brocades and florals used sparingly.

Each season, Alan's inspiration comes from somewhere new, but his collections always manage to stay true to their roots. His brand is based in New York and he looks to the city constantly for ideas and updates. The easy-feeling, American-inspired classics that have garnered Steven Alan a loyal following remain a touchstone for his ever-growing brand.

1994 Opens first store in New York
1999 Begins designing his own line, starting with the men's button-down shirt
2008 Steven Alan becomes bicoastal, with six stores in New York and three in Southern California
2011 Stages his first Fashion Week presentation
2012 Opens his second store in San Francisco, making that his eleventh store in the United States

Steven Alan, 2011

1943 First New York Fashion Week

1953 French actress Isabelle Huppert is born

1956–59 Guggenheim Museum
constructed in New York

1974 Malcolm McLaren and
Vivienne Westwood
open their boutique
SEX in London

| 1930 | 1935 | 1940 | 1945 | 1950 | 1955 | 1960 | 1965 | 1970 | 1975 | 1980 |

Sarah Burton for Alexander McQueen
Fall/Winter 2011/12 Prêt-à-Porter show, Paris

1985 Live Aid charity concert for famine relief in Africa

1991 The World Wide Web made publicly available

2004 Founding of Facebook

2011 Royal wedding of Prince William of Wales and Catherine Middleton

2018 Winter Olympic Games in Pyeongchang, South Korea

1985 1990 1995 2000 2005 2010 2015 2020 2025 2030 2035

SARAH BURTON

It took a tragedy to catapult her to fame, but Sarah Burton has proved herself a worthy successor to the Alexander McQueen name. Following McQueen's suicide in 2010, Burton was named creative director of the British, Gucci-owned brand.

She was no newcomer to the company, though, having started with McQueen as an intern while still in school at the Central Saint Martins College of Art and Design in London. Upon graduating, she began working full time as Alexander McQueen's personal assistant and within three years was promoted to the head of womenswear. In that role, Burton worked closely with the designer to create his collections as well as dresses for some of the world's most famous women—Lady Gaga, Gwyneth Paltrow, and Michelle Obama among them.

Her designs have distinct elements of the McQueen we all came to know and love—he did, after all, teach her the craft—but her style is more feminine and, often, considered more wearable. For her first collection as creative director, presented in Paris in October 2010, many were surprised by the lightness of the clothes, though the familiar exaggerated silhouettes of her predecessor remained. Burton also did away with extravagant set design and instead gave a more stripped-down presentation, her runway made of simple floorboards with grass coming up between them. The thirty-five looks, a mix of colorful brocade, butterfly prints, and tailored waistcoats, were received extremely well and Sarah Burton was accepted as the heir to McQueen.

Her fame was cemented on April 29, 2011, when it was revealed, after much secrecy, that Kate Middleton had chosen Burton to design her wedding dress. The dress, a long-sleeved ivory silk-and-lace gown, was the perfect mix of tradition and modernity, fitting for the twenty-nine-year-old Duchess of Cambridge who had updated much of the royal wedding ceremony. The V-neck design looked youthful and elegant, while the traditional lacework was appropriate for the event. Philippa Middleton (aka Pippa), Kate's sister and maid of honor, wore a dress designed by Burton, as well. The form-fitting ivory gown had a draped cowl neck and lace trims that matched the bride. The dresses were praised by most, and with over three billion worldwide viewers,

the royal wedding served to turn designer Sarah Burton into a household name. By the time she attended the Metropolitan Museum of Art gala for the opening of the Alexander McQueen exhibition in early May 2011, she was a star in her own right.

Sarah Burton was born and raised in Manchester and currently lives with her fashion-photographer husband, David Burton. Her parents have said that their daughter's artistic ability was evident from childhood and that she always loved fashion. They, like the rest of the world, only speculated that their daughter was designing Kate Middleton's dress, the secrecy so intense that it was rumored only fifteen McQueen employees were allowed to work on it.

In the months following the royal wedding, Burton began work on her third collection for Spring 2012. The collection proved two things: first, that the Alexander McQueen aesthetic lives on in Sarah Burton (evidenced by a series of black leather looks); but secondly, that Burton has carved out her own vision as a designer. Her Spring 2012 collection was inspired by the ocean—dresses in shades of pale coral and shimmering gold, oyster prints on silk chiffon, dresses encrusted with mother-of-pearl. Like the pastel-heavy palette, the shapes were feminized, too, with raised waists emphasized by belts and rows of Empire ruffles. It was Gaia, the mythological Greek Earth mother that served as Burton's inspiration, the beaded dresses and cascading ruffles meant to conjure the wonder of nature and the sea. The almost couture-like pieces were extolled by many, including Emmanuelle Alt, the editor-in-chief of French *Vogue*, who, according to journalists, fell to the feet of the designer backstage after the show, praising her work. While Burton continues to invoke the style and spirit of her former boss and mentor, she has, in a short period of time, developed Alexander McQueen into a brand, evolving the look of the house with her own extraordinary designs.

1974 Born in Prestbury, Cheshire, England
1993 Moves to London to study print fashion at Central Saint Martins
1996 Interns for Alexander McQueen
1997 Graduates from Central Saint Martins and joins Alexander McQueen
2000 Becomes head of womenswear at Alexander McQueen
2010 Becomes creative director at Alexander McQueen
2011 Designs Kate Middleton's wedding dress; wins British Fashion Awards' Designer of the Year
2012 Wins Elle Style Awards' International Designer of the Year

Sarah Burton, 2011

left
The wedding dress of Catherine,
the Duchess of Cambridge, at
Buckingham Palace, London,
2011

right
Sarah Burton for Alexander
McQueen Fall/Winter 2012/13
Prêt-à-Porter show, Paris

1953 Hubert de Givenchy meets
Audrey Hepburn

1942 Edward Hopper paints
Nighthawks

1961 Founding of Amnesty International

1974 Beverly Johnson appears
as the first black model
on the cover of American
Vogue

1930	1935	1940	1945	1950	1955	1960	1965	1970	1975	1980

Joseph Altuzarra Fall/Winter 2012/13 show,
New York

1989 George H. W. Bush sworn
in as 41st US president

2008 Pop artist Robert Rauschenberg dies

1995 eBay founded

2002 Womenswear and accessories
brand Proenza Schouler
founded in New York

1982 Michael Jackson releases
his album *Thriller*

| 1985 | 1990 | 1995 | 2000 | 2005 | 2010 | 2015 | 2020 | 2025 | 2030 | 2035 |

JOSEPH ALTUZARRA

With influences that stem from both the classic legacy of Paris fashion and the ever-evolving energy of New York, Altuzarra is a fashion label that combines practicality with luxury. The label's ambitious young designer, Joseph Altuzarra, has successfully developed his feminine, imaginative label—all before turning thirty.

Designer Joseph Altuzarra was born in 1984 in Paris to a Chinese American mother and a French Basque father. He moved to the United States for university, studying art history at Swarthmore College in Pennsylvania. On a whim, he sent his resume to Marc Jacobs and landed an internship with the designer, prompting him to move to New York. Following the six-month internship, Altuzarra landed a design assistant position at Proenza Schouler. In 2006, the young designer was recruited by Givenchy to go to Paris as a design assistant for the house. Altuzarra accepted, but decided to return to New York two years later to launch his own line.

His fifteen-piece debut at New York Fashion Week was in February 2009. The twenty-five-year-old designer showed a polished and incredibly professional fall collection, much to the pleasure of editors, critics, and buyers alike. His starting points were the forties and the eighties, a mix of tailored day jackets and body-conscious, ruched dresses. His last three looks were tight, one-shoulder dresses in a metallic silk lamé worn with over-the-knee black boots—a perfect blend of sexy and tough.

For his Fall 2011 collection, Altuzarra moved away from the precisely tailored, structured pieces of his previous collections, inspired this season by grunge and the nineties. A series of oversized military parkas paired with silk slip dresses opened the show, a look inspired by old photos of Kate Moss wearing a similar style. "I wanted something longer and looser, something sensual and feminine, but utilitarian at the same time," said the designer. The impressive outerwear, which ranged from parkas to trenches to capes, showed another, very talented side of Altuzarra. Not surprisingly, the utility parkas sold out on Net-A-Porter the day they became available. So, it made complete sense when Altuzarra, with a business that was not yet three years old, was announced as the 2011 CFDA/Vogue Fashion Fund winner in November of that year, with a prize of $300,000 to enable him to pursue his design plans.

For Spring 2012, Altuzarra showed a sport-inspired collection. With his statement nylon windbreakers and quilted leather jackets, Altuzarra proved, once again, that outerwear was one of his major strengths. There were elements of baseball and scuba, with distinctively Hawaiian prints. A white leather dress with long sleeves, for instance, featured a bold, tropical-print panel down the center and a crisp blazer was updated in a green floral. Altuzarra's spring collection was precisely on-trend, with a mix of streetwear-inspired pieces and bold looks.

All-around an ambitious designer, Altuzarra outdid himself for Fall 2012, with his most successful collection to date. His inspiration was the sailor/adventurer Corto Maltese, a comic book character from the sixties. The swashbuckling Maltese appeared on the runway in the form of military coats, velvet blazers, flared corduroy pants, fur vests, and thigh-high boots. From Maltese's travels in Morocco and India, Altuzarra added in heavily decorated gypsy dresses with colorful embroidery and medallions. The designer also brought back some of his signature looks, such as a ruched jersey dress similar to the lamé pieces from 2009. The collection was the perfect mix of wearable clothes—including several incredibly chic black dresses and coats—and high-concept looks favored by fashion editors.

"I just wanted to do things that women want to wear," Altuzarra said, "to figure out how to make clothes that look rich but feel easy." The statement may have been in regards to his Fall 2012 collection, but it holds true for each season that he designs. Joseph Altuzarra may be young, but his impeccable design concepts and his clarity of vision suggest that he is anything but inexperienced.

1984 Born in Paris
2005 Graduates with a BA in Art and Art History from Swarthmore College at the University of Philadelphia
2005–06 Moves to New York; interns at Marc Jacobs Studio; freelances at Proenza Schouler
2006 Hired as Riccardo Tisci's first assistant at Givenchy in Paris
2008 Returns to New York and launches own line, ALTUZARRA
2009 Debuts his line at New York Fashion Week
2011 Wins the CFDA/Vogue Fashion Fund Award

Joseph Altuzarra, 2011

1949 Elsa Schiaparelli opens a branch of
her fashion house in New York

1963 James Brown's breakthrough album
Live at the Apollo

1976 Founding of
The Body Shop

1973 First commercial PC

1930   1935   1940   1945   1950   1955   1960   1965   1970   1975   1980

Yigal Azrouël Fall/Winter 2012/13 collection

1989 First electronic dance music festival Love Parade in Berlin

1995 *Toy Story* is the first wholly computer-generated film

1987 *The Bonfire of the Vanities* by Tom Wolfe is published

2009 Barack Obama sworn in as 44th US president

2012 Whitney Houston dies

1985	1990	1995	2000	2005	2010	2015	2020	2025	2030	2035

YIGAL AZROUËL

Yigal Azrouël, who is of French Moroccan descent, is a designer of choice for the New York society set. His effortlessly stylish and flattering designs are consistently on-trend without being complicated or hard to wear.

Azrouël was raised in Ashdod, Israel, one of eight children born to a sneaker manufacturer. He served in the Israeli army in the early 1990s, where he would fill journals with fashion sketches of dresses. After leaving the military, Azrouël spent time traveling, looking through flea markets for vintage scarves, a style element that he has since incorporated into his signature look. Eventually, Azrouël arrived in Paris and through some family connections, received a ticket to a Christian Dior fashion show. It was there, said the designer, he knew he wanted to work in the industry. With that goal in mind, the twenty-two-year-old Azrouël moved to the United States, staying with an aunt in Washington, D.C. and draping mannequins in his free time. Within a few years, he moved to New York and began working on his line.

Yigal Azrouël's eponymous label debuted in 1998 and throughout the next few years the designer's career took off. By 2004, he had opened a showroom and production space in the Garment District, a boutique in the Meatpacking District, and had been inducted into the CFDA. In 2007, Azrouël added a full menswear collection, as well as a line of accessories. While his business grew, Azrouël's refined and wearable clothes had also been getting attention in the media, his pieces worn on *Sex and the City* and featured in the pages of *Vogue*.

By the end of the decade, Azrouël had become known for his dresses, along with his affinity for clean lines and draped layers. His signature look, one of ease and accessibility, is not avant-garde. "I don't design for celebrities. I think about what looks good on real women with real bodies," the designer has said. For his Spring 2012 collection, Azrouël focused on simple silhouettes and a palette of neutrals—tans, grays, blacks, and whites—along with a vibrant rainbow of bold colors, including red, orange, yellow, green, and blue. His looks paired wide-leg trousers with simply cut long-sleeve blouses and long collarless coats worn over primary

color suits. There were several dresses, too, including a high-necked yellow look that banded at the waist and cascaded to the floor with one suggestive slit that revealed just the right amount of leg. For day, there was a kelly-green polo dress with short sleeves and a fitted silhouette. The simple shapes were infused with the perfect amount of sexiness, proving that Azrouël not only knew how to interpret trends, but also knew just what his customer would want to wear each season.

In February 2012, just before Azrouël showed his Fall 2012 collection, he opened a second store in Manhattan, this time for his contemporary, lower-priced line, Cut 25. He launched Cut 25 in 2010, envisioning a more youthful counterpart to his principal line. The trendy minidresses, T-shirts, and leather jackets, which are often sold in bright colors and splashy prints, are meant for layering. "I felt like the contemporary market was missing something," the designer said, "There wasn't anything with that heat, that's sexy, but also cool and chic at the same time."

Not only does Azrouël dress the young, wealthy circles of New York women, but he socializes with them as well. For years, the designer has been linked to several Manhattan socialites, perhaps positioning him at a place to better understand what they want as consumers. Yigal Azrouël's on-trend yet accessible approach to fashion has made him the gold standard for women that crave effortless, chic style.

1973 Born in Israel
1995 Moves to New York
1998 Launches first collection In New York
2000 Opens full-service showroom and production facility in the garment district of New York; shows at New York Fashion Week
2003 Opens first freestanding boutique in New York's Meatpacking District
2004 Inducted into the Council of Fashion Designers of America (CFDA); first international presentation at the Ritz Paris
2009 Chosen as the featured designer at New York Fashion Week
2010 Launches younger line, Cut 25
2011 Debuts shoe collection; featured designer at Milan's Spiga2 store

Yigal Azrouël, 2011

1943 First French "fashion week" is held

1956 Elvis Presley releases
"Heartbreak Hotel," his first big hit

1962 Andy Warhol's first New York solo
Pop Art exhibition at Stable Gallery

1975 Microsoft is founded
in Albuquerque,
New Mexico

| 1930 | 1935 | 1940 | 1945 | 1950 | 1955 | 1960 | 1965 | 1970 | 1975 | 1980 |

Balenciaga Fall/Winter 2008/09 collection,
Paris Fashion Week

2003 Jean Paul Gaultier becomes
creative director of Hermès

1984 Prince releases his album
Purple Rain

1997 James Cameron's *Titanic* is
released in theaters

2010 The Burj Khalifa in Dubai is
officially opened

2001 The Gucci Group buys Balenciaga

| 1985 | 1990 | 1995 | 2000 | 2005 | 2010 | 2015 | 2020 | 2025 | 2030 | 2035 |

NICHOLAS GHESQUIÈRE

When Nicholas Ghesquière was plucked out of obscurity in 1997, no one could've guessed that he'd become one of the world's most influential contemporary designers. Now, at Balenciaga, Ghesquière's structural, modern aesthetic has become a driving force in the fashion industry.

During his reign as the creative director at Balenciaga, Ghesquière has given the brand a hard-edged, yet feminine, precision. While his work frequently references and pays homage to Cristobal Balenciaga, the Basque designer who founded the brand in 1918, Ghesquière's vision is entirely his own.

Born in 1971 in Comines, Nord-Pas de Calais, France, Ghesquière grew up in Loudun, Vienne. From a young age, Ghesquière was sketching designs and creating dresses from curtains and other materials he found around the house. At fourteen, he interned with French designer Agnès b, and after school, from 1990 to 1992, he assisted Jean Paul Gaultier. In 1995, Ghesquière joined Balenciaga as a licensed product designer, of which he said, "It was not the most exciting job but for me it was the most beautiful name in fashion…. it was interesting to work on this license and to see what was left from Balenciaga." Two years later, he was appointed the new creative director.

When Ghesquière took control at Balenciaga, the house had fallen out of the public eye, but in just a few short years he revived the brand, renewing the interest of not only the fashion press, but also Balenciaga's loyal following. In 2001, the Gucci Group purchased Balenciaga, adding the label to their roster of luxury brands. By the time Ghesquière showed his Fall 2001 collection in Paris, he had already been dubbed "fashion's new messiah." The black and gray collection was influenced by the early twentieth century, infused with the designer's own sculptural silhouettes. Ghesquière also scored with his accessories, creating, in 2001, the Lariat bag. That same year he won the CFDA's International Award for best womenswear designer.

Ghesquière's success at Balenciaga only continued, delving, each season, into an exploration of structured silhouettes as well as into the exclusive archives of the house. Of his Spring 2008 collection he said, "I'm exploring new territory, within the references of the house…. I've done prints before,

but I never went to the flowers." The flowers—pansies, daffodils, hydrangeas—were explosive, but the shapes were sharp and hard. The outfits were unlike anything showing in fashion at that time, adding yet again to the genius of Ghesquière.

For the following fall, Ghesquière "wanted something austere, but with a bit of Spanish drama." The result was a melding of historical Balenciaga references and Ghesquière's high-tech fabrics of plastic and latex. The molded black dresses were an update on a fifties cocktail look, but with sharp lines, high slit skirts, and the designer's signature curved hips. Draped velvet tops in bright jewel tones were shown with skinny pants, while sculpted latex jackets doubled as eveningwear, albeit of the futuristic variety.

For Spring 2012, Ghesquière pushed his silhouette further, employing traditional couture construction to his updated looks. Voluminous dresses were comprised of panels of patchworked fabrics and color-blocked jackets with exaggerated shoulders were paired with barely-there short shorts. Cristobal Balenciaga's influence was present in the shapes, prints, and haute-couture technique, but Ghesquière pushed the proportions, the fabrics, and the silhouettes straight into the twenty-first century.

Nicholas Ghesquière has reinvented the House of Balenciaga, infusing the label with a modern edge and an unquestionably cool femininity. Ghesquière's success can be credited, in a large part, to his frequent nods to Cristobal Balenciaga, which he combines seamlessly with his architectural silhouettes and experimental fabrics. For over a decade, Ghesquière has remained one of the strongest forces in fashion, designing clothes, as he says, "for a woman who is looking to the future." It is fitting then that the fashion world at large impatiently awaits the next season of Balenciaga, eager to see what Nicholas Ghesquière will do next.

1971 Born in Comines, France
1990–92 Works as assistant at Jean Paul Gaultier
1995 Hired to design for Balenciaga's parent company
1997 Becomes creative director of Balenciaga
1998 Madonna wears his design to the Golden Globe Awards
2000 Named Best Avant-Garde Designer at VH1/Vogue Fashion Awards
2001 Wins CFDA International Award
2002 First collection presented at the Gagosian Gallery
2003 Opens boutique in New York's Chelsea
2008 Receives Accessories Council Excellence Award for Designer of the Year
2010 First freestanding Balenciaga men's store opens on the Parisian Left Bank

Nicolas Ghesquière

Balenciaga Fall/Winter 2010/11 collection,
Paris Fashion Week

Balenciaga Spring/Summer 2008
collection, Paris Fashion Week

1943 Premiere of *Casablanca*, directed
by Michael Curtiz

1955 First Documenta exhibition
in Kassel

1964 Jean-Luc Godard's nouvelle-vague
film *Bande à part* is released

1979 Sony
begins
selling
the
Walkman

1930	1935	1940	1945	1950	1955	1960	1965	1970	1975	1980

Band Of Outsiders Fall 2010 show,
Mercedes-Benz Fashion Week, New York

1988 Christian Lacroix presents his first prêt-à-porter collection

1998 Google is founded

2008 Tom Ford directs the film *A Single Man*

2018 Winter Olympic Games in Sochi, Russia

1994 First issue of *Vice* magazine is published

1985 1990 1995 2000 2005 2010 2015 2020 2025 2030 2035

SCOTT STERNBERG

With Band of Outsiders, Scott Sternberg has recontextualized American classics with his updated twists on menswear and tailoring. Growing up in Dayton, Ohio, Scott Sternberg says he "stuck out like a sore thumb," but the designer's keen aesthetic has given way to three successful lines for men and women.

As the child of a family that loved to shop, Sternberg would dress in head-to-toe Ralph Lauren, but despite his youthful sartorial leanings he didn't wind up in fashion right away. For five years Sternberg worked at Creative Artists Agency, one of Hollywood's biggest talent agencies, but left the firm in 2003 to become an independent brand consultant, working with Target and other companies. Shortly after, he discovered an ability to make clothes. "It wasn't like I felt I had a calling for, you know, *fashion*," he said. "I just wanted to make a great shirt and a great tie for myself. I don't know why, but that was the instinct and I thought I could do it." He began with a classic: the oxford shirt. "I took an old oxford-cloth button-down, put it on a bust form, and started taking it in every which way and reconstructing it." The result was a surprise hit and soon major retailers were lining up to stock Sternberg's new line, Band of Outsiders.

The name Band of Outsiders comes from the English title of Jean-Luc Godard's 1964 film *Bande à part*. For his label, Sternberg, a film buff and Godard fan, acts not only as designer, but also as the image-maker, shooting the line's seasonal lookbooks himself on a Polaroid camera. What began as a cost-effective way to produce imagery for his young company became a consistent thread in Band of Outsiders' visuals. Since that first Polaroid photo shoot, the company's photos have featured actors and actresses such as Marisa Tomei, Kirsten Dunst, Jason Schwartzman, Michelle Williams, and, most recently, artist Ed Ruscha. The celebrity following is evident at Band of Outsiders' New York fashion shows, too, where boldfaced names such as Kanye West and Aziz Ansari sit front row.

But it was a lot more than celebrity friends that launched Band of Outsiders. In 2004, when Sternberg showed his first collection of sample shirts and ties to buyers from Barneys and Jeffrey, the stores were quick to pick up the new line, acknowledging that it filled a very real hole in the market. That hole was for classic Americana-inspired pieces and a nostalgic take on preppy dressing. Within just a couple of years, Sternberg was able to begin designing his own fabrics with specialty mills and work with famed Brooklyn-based tailor Martin Greenfield on handmade suits.

With Band of Outsiders selling well, Sternberg launched Boy by Band of Outsiders in 2007. The menswear-inspired Boy centers on reinterpreting men's pieces for women, such as perfectly shrunken blazers or tailored trousers. Then, for Spring 2011, Sternberg added another line, Girl by Band of Outsiders. Girl's first collection was unabashedly feminine, with classically draped Grecian-style dresses and a light, summery palette with delicate prints.

For his Fall 2012 show, Sternberg's inspiration came from South of the Border. His Mexican reference was seen in the desert colors and the alpaca sweaters that showed on the runway. His menswear included preppy embroidery on suits alongside sporty puffer vests and patterned scarves. The menswear was heavily referenced in Boy, with similar colors and a consistent Mexican theme, plus some sleek and sexy black tuxedo-inspired dresses that came out at the end. Girl, however, was soft and feminine with long, flowing skirts, tiny floral-print dresses, and several cozy hand-knits.

With three lines under the Band of Outsiders umbrella, Scott Sternberg has created a company with something for everyone. Though his clothing is not avant-garde or particularly cutting edge, the Los Angeles-based designer is truly an undeniable force in American fashion, playing with preppy nostalgia and slightly twisted takes on sophisticated feminine dressing.

2004 Founds Band of Outsiders in January; shows first collection of sample shirts and ties to buyers from Barneys and Jeffrey

2006 Collaborates with tailor Martin Greenfield

2007 Introduces Boy by Band of Outsiders

2009 Wins the CFDA award for Menswear Designer of the Year

2011 Launches Girl by Band of Outsiders, a more feminine collection of separates

2012 Band of Outsiders stages the "longest fashion show ever" (sixty hours) at Paris Men's Fashion Week

Scott Sternberg, 2011

1949 Premiere of Arthur Miller's play
Death of a Salesman

1961 *Breakfast at Tiffany's* starring
Audrey Hepburn is released
in theaters

1971 MoMA PS1 is established

| 1930 | 1935 | 1940 | 1945 | 1950 | 1955 | 1960 | 1965 | 1970 | 1975 | 1980 |

Victoria by Victoria Beckham Fall 2012 show,
Mercedes-Benz Fashion Week, New York

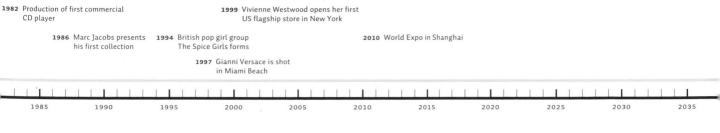

1982 Production of first commercial
CD player

1986 Marc Jacobs presents
his first collection

1999 Vivienne Westwood opens her first
US flagship store in New York

1994 British pop girl group
The Spice Girls forms

1997 Gianni Versace is shot
in Miami Beach

2010 World Expo in Shanghai

1985   1990   1995   2000   2005   2010   2015   2020   2025   2030   2035

VICTORIA BECKHAM

From pop star to footballer's wife to fashion designer, Victoria Beckham has had many lives. As a designer, Beckham has cultivated a sophisticated signature style that revolves around a fitted, body-conscious silhouette.

The designer was born in 1974 in Hertfordshire, England into a very wealthy family (rumor has it that as a girl, Victoria Beckham, née Adams, hated being driven to school in her father's Rolls-Royce). It was fitting, then, that as she rose to fame with British pop girl group the Spice Girls she became known as Posh Spice. She was in college in 1994 when she answered an ad in a magazine and auditioned for the band, and by 1996 their single "Wannabe" was a number-one hit in over thirty countries. They quickly became international superstars, releasing several albums over the next few years. By the end of 2000, when the Spice Girls disbanded, Beckham was already married to famous footballer David Beckham, and the two had a young son, Brooklyn.

It wasn't until the early 2000s that Victoria Beckham entered the fashion world, first as a brand ambassador for Dolce & Gabbana and the face of Rocawear and then, in 2004, as the designer of a limited-edition line for Rock & Republic called VB Rocks. Over the following years, Beckham found herself in other roles with the fashion industry: as a model for Roberto Cavalli and as Katie Holmes' stylist for the March 2006 issue of *Harper's Bazaar*. In September of that year she launched her own denim line, dVb Style, as well as a his-and-hers fragrance line, Intimately Beckham. Then, in 2008, at New York Fashion Week, Beckham debuted her own eponymous line. The fifteen dresses, which she showed in exclusive appointments at the Waldorf Astoria, were met with stellar reviews. Ranging in price from $1,500 to $3,600, the fitted, body-conscious pieces all hit just below the knee, a style favored by Beckham. "I don't want to make dresses that will date," said the designer of that first collection, the goal instead was to make flattering, timeless pieces with special details to improve posture and enhance curves.

For her Spring 2010 presentation, Beckham maintained her signature sex appeal while delving into some new territory. "I wanted to push myself,"

Beckham said, "to play with new silhouettes, textures, and print." For the collection, Beckham added peplum skirts, angular strapless bodices, paneled shoulders, and an abstract, graphic print on two looser-fitting shapes. Her five evening dresses were the collection's biggest hit, with bands of black at the waist and bodice that gave a slimming effect.

For Spring 2012, Beckham unveiled a new line, Victoria, Victoria Beckham. Already the mother of three boys, Beckham designed this line while pregnant with her fourth child and her first daughter. Victoria, Victoria Beckham is not only younger and girlier than her main line, but also significantly less expensive, with dresses retailing for well under $1,000. The launch collection was inspired by Emily the Strange, an edgy, adolescent cartoon character who is followed around by four cats. The looser silhouettes, sixties design details, and whimsical prints of Victoria were the perfect foil to the glamorous, evening looks represented by Victoria Beckham.

For Fall 2012, Beckham maintained her long and lean silhouette, infusing the collection with sportier elements, such as contrasted polo collars, bold black stripes, and cheerleader skirts. Victoria, Victoria Beckham also stayed true to its charming whimsy, with swan prints on collars, mod shapes, and vibrant colorblocking.

Beckham has said on several occasions that if she herself doesn't want to wear it, she won't make it. And, true to her word, the celebrity designer is frequently photographed in her looks from both lines. With a natural talent for designing flattering, sophisticated dresses, Beckham has earned respect from the fashion industry and consumers alike. It's hard to imagine that Beckham, with her signature design style and impressive sales, was known to the world as Posh Spice just ten years ago. With her remarkable talent and knack for reinvention, who knows what the next decade will hold for Victoria Beckham.

1974 Born in Goffs Oak, Hertfordshire, England
1996–2001 Member of the Spice Girls
2003 Named brand ambassador for Dolce & Gabbana
2004–06 Co-designs for Rock and Republic
2006 Launches her own denim line, dVb Style
2008 Debuts her line Victoria Beckham
2009 Featured on the cover of Russian *Vogue*
2011 Introduces secondary label, Victoria by Victoria Beckham

Victoria Beckham, 2012

left
Victoria Beckham, Color Block Cap
Fitted Dress, Spring/Summer 2012
collection

right
Victoria Beckham, Scoop-Neck Floor-
Length Dress (left) and Pocket-Front
Floor-Length Dress, 2012

1942 Peggy Guggenheim opens her Art of
this Century Gallery in New York

1959 Miles Davis releases the
album *Kind of Blue*

1969 Stonewall Uprising
on Christopher
Street in New York

1977 Yohji Yamamoto
presents his first
collection in
Tokyo

1930   1935   1940   1945   1950   1955   1960   1965   1970   1975   1980

Chris Benz Fall/Winter 2010/11
presentation, New York

CHRIS BENZ

Born in Seattle, Chris Benz presented his first ready-to-wear collection in 2007, at the young age of twenty-four. His designs are rooted in classic American sportswear with inventive twists on the classics and a deft use of color and prints.

Growing up in Seattle, Benz spent his childhood discovering antique jewelry and dolls from the fifties in his grandmother's attic, and says he was "that kid who didn't subscribe to what everyone else was wearing." "I used to sit in bed at night and flip through design-school catalogues," says Benz of his teenage years. "I found out that Parsons accepted a small number of high school juniors, so I applied my sophomore year and got in." He left for New York to pursue his design studies at age seventeen. Before he graduated from Parsons in 2004, he was awarded the coveted CFDA Emerging Designer Award. While in school, Benz interned at Marc Jacobs and upon graduation he landed a design position at J. Crew, where he stayed until the launch of his own line three years later.

He staged his first presentation during New York Fashion Week in February 2007, in one of Christie's art galleries. Benz's color palette stole the show, with pairings such as bright blue and rust, gray-blue and mustard. The look was preppy, yet polished, with just the right amount of quirk. The outerwear—pea coats, trenches, and tweed—were paired with jodhpurs, pajama tops, and wool shorts. Benz's breakout show was met with strong reviews, as was his sophomore collection, which showed six months later. The second presentation was inspired by a fictional 1930s starlet, restless and playing dress-up in her metallic jacquard suits and slouchy jersey gowns. Once again, the designer displayed his confidence with color, creating three scenarios of models, arranged by hue. The hot pinks mixed with oranges and mustard yellows, the greens ran the gamut from pastel mint to acid, and the blues came in jeweled cobalt and electric turquoise.

For his Spring 2009 show, Benz still looked to the past for inspiration, but his pieces felt completely contemporary. "I looked at Revolutionary War-era dressing," the young designer said, "but interpreted it in supermodern fabrics." The military jackets, which were fitted and slightly cropped, came in

white, a light green-gray, and a bright poppy orange. For his first full runway show, the designer showed a range of colors, though with slightly more muted hues than in previous seasons. His classic silhouettes had a definitively modern spirit and no lack of special details.

Channeling nostalgia and referencing the classics is what Benz does best. For Spring 2012 the concept was "Andy Warhol's superstars go to Coney Island, with a nod to candy kids." The trippy black-and-white graphic prints and the bright pinks, oranges, and lime greens certainly got the point across. The shapes, however, were significantly more reserved, with skirts below the knee and covered up necklines. He followed up with a fall collection that spoke to the classic glamour of days past. "I remember sitting in my mom's bathroom, watching her get all dolled up while listening to *The Judy Garland Holiday Special*," said the designer. "And now girls are making the effort to be glam like that again." Complete with wigs, hats, gloves, and fur collars, Benz's girl this season was ladylike and playful. Tulle petticoats popped out from under fifties-style dresses and fur pullovers were paired with feminine cigarette pants. The glamour escalated with the eveningwear, including a floor-length gunmetal-silver gown encrusted with sequins.

Season after season, it's clear that those childhood days spent with the antique treasures of his grandmother's attic made an impression. Benz's ability to transform his influences and nostalgic references into wearable, modern pieces is what gives his clothing its charm. The Chris Benz girl, as he puts it, is an "ageless sophisticate," someone who conveys a sense of history as well as progress and fresh modernity.

1982 Born in Seattle on September 20
1999 Moves to New York to study at Parsons School of Design; interns with Marc Jacobs
2004 Graduates from Parsons, receives the CFDA Emerging Designer Award
2005 Designer for Dresses and Special Occasion at J. Crew
2007 Presents first ready-to-wear collection at New York Fashion Week
2009 Inducted into the Council of Fashion Designers of America (CFDA)
2011 Michelle Obama begins wearing his line

Chris Benz

left
Chris Benz Spring 2012 presentation,
Mercedes Benz Fashion Week, New York

right
Chris Benz Fall 2012 presentation,
Mercedes-Benz Fashion Week, New York

1960 The Beatles form

1955 Burberry is taken over by
Great Universal Stores

1973 Vogue becomes a monthly
publication

1930 1935 1940 1945 1950 1955 1960 1965 1970 1975 1980

Burberry Prorsum Spring/Summer
2012 show, London Fashion Week

1988 The exhibition *Freeze* in London
leads to the breakthrough of the
Young British Artists

2005 Founding of YouTube

1995 Launch of the Japanese electronic
toy Tamagotchi

2011 Amy Winehouse dies

2006 Frida Giannini becomes
creative director of Gucci

1987 Phuture releases the single "Acid Tracks,"
giving birth to the acid house movement

1985 1990 1995 2000 2005 2010 2015 2020 2025 2030 2035

CHRISTOPHER BAILEY

In London, Burberry is the biggest game in town, and since 2001 Christopher Bailey has been running the show as the company's chief creative officer. Bailey's effortlessly cool looks and modern updates to the brand's classic pieces have made him a true force in the fashion world.

The title positions Bailey at the head of a large fashion empire, designing all of the label's collections including Burberry Prorsum, Burberry London, Thomas Burberry, and the globally licensed products. His title encompasses more than just design however, as Bailey is responsible for the company's overall image, including advertising, store design, and visuals. Burberry, founded in 1856, is now listed as one of the ten most valuable luxury brands in the world, thanks in large part to Bailey's transformation.

Christopher Bailey was born in 1971 in West Yorkshire, England. After receiving his degree from the Royal College of Art and spending just over a year designing for Donna Karan, he was hired by Tom Ford as a senior womenswear designer for Gucci. After six years at the Italian company, Bailey landed back in England at Burberry, where, ten years later, he has turned the classic brand into a fashion phenomenon. His brilliance, and success, with the brand lies in his ability to not only reconcile tradition and modernity, but in his understanding of how women want to dress. Each season Bailey combines the company's classics with modern twists to achieve an effortlessly cool, updated look. The trench coat, a staple and financial cornerstone for Burberry, is always represented in seasonal collections, staying true to the company's heritage. But Bailey, understanding that in order to grow there needs to be change, always includes tweaks to the classics with updates to the color palette (trenches in army green or deep purple) or by adding details such as a luxurious fur collar.

Coats, as well, have become a big business for Burberry thanks to Bailey. For the Fall 2010 collection, Bailey paraded a string of large-collared shearlings and military-inspired parkas down the runway. His oversized, cropped flight jackets caused an instant stir, with glowing reviews and a slew of imitations. The overall look was authentically cool, a pairing of strong, masculine jackets with feminine lace dresses. This was sex appeal for the twenty-first century.

The Fall 2010 show was revolutionary for other reasons, as well, securing Christopher Bailey's position as a leader in the fashion industry. In addition to the runway show, the presentation was live-streamed globally and screened in 3-D for private groups of invited guests in New York, Los Angeles, Tokyo, and Dubai. Billed as the world's first truly global fashion show, the Fall 2010 Burberry show reached an estimated hundred million viewers. But perhaps the most brilliant move of all was the new technology that allowed customers to purchase items from the runway just moments after the show finished. For seventy-two short hours, those coveted shearling jackets and other fall runway pieces were available to order, whipping the fashion world into a buying frenzy and leaving competitors in the technological dust.

Bailey's contributions to the industry have not gone unnoticed. The designer has won several awards for his work, including Designer of the Year at the British Fashion Awards in 2005 and 2009 and the prestigious International Award from the Council of Fashion Designers of America (CFDA) in 2010. In addition to his effortlessly chic designs, Bailey's work for Burberry is immortalized in the company's ad campaigns. Featuring top British models, such as Kate Moss and Lily Donaldson, and more emerging faces, such as actress Emma Watson and socialite Cara Delevingne, the Burberry name has become synonymous with cool British style. The classic Burberry look always remains, but thanks to Christopher Bailey, the company remains a leader in today's fashion industry.

1971 Born in Halifax, West Yorkshire, England

1990 Graduates from the University of Westminster; named student of the year at graduate fashion week

1994 Graduates with a master's degree from London's Royal College of Art; moves to New York City to design for Donna Karan

1996–2001 Named senior designer of womenswear for Tom Ford at Gucci in Milan

2001 Replaces Roberto Menichetti as creative director of Burberry

2005 Wins Designer of the Year at the British Fashion Awards

2008 Establishes the Burberry Foundation

2009 Appointed chief creative officer of Burberry; British Fashion Council's Designer of the Year; appointed a Member of the Order of the British Empire for contributions to the fashion industry

2010 Wins CFDA International Award and British Fashion Council's Digital Innovation Award

2011 Holds holographic runway show in Beijing

Christopher Bailey, 2008

Burberry Prorsum Fall/Winter 2012/13 show,
London Fashion Week

1945 The House of Carven is founded

1955 *The Family of Man* exhibition at the Museum of Modern Art in New York

1968 Premiere of Stanley Kubrick's *2001: A Space Odyssey*

1969 Woodstock Festival

1978 Forming of the band Duran Duran

1930 · 1935 · 1940 · 1945 · 1950 · 1955 · 1960 · 1965 · 1970 · 1975 · 1980

Carven Fall/Winter 2012/13 Prêt-à-Porter show, Paris Fashion Week

1981 First issue of *i-D* magazine
is published

1989 First electronic dance music
festival Love Parade in Berlin

2001 First same-sex marriage
in the Netherlands

2009 Barack Obama awarded
Nobel Peace Price

| 1985 | 1990 | 1995 | 2000 | 2005 | 2010 | 2015 | 2020 | 2025 | 2030 | 2035 |

GUILLAUME HENRY

Guillaume Henry has a very clear idea of the girl who dresses in Carven: she is young, smart, cool, and enjoys wearing a short skirt. The considerable charm of Carven, which has been evident since Henry revived the line for Spring 2010, is thanks, in large part, to the considerable charm of the designer himself.

The House of Carven was founded in 1945 and was, in its heyday, most famous for its signature perfume, Ma Griffe. For years, the house, a member of the Chambre Syndicale de la Haute Couture, made haute-couture pieces for a very exclusive clientele. In 2009, the owner of Carven called Guillaume Henry, who suggested the house move away from haute couture and begin designing for real women. Henry was quickly installed as the creative director and the house was relaunched as a ready-to-wear label.

Guillaume Henry began his career at Givenchy in 2005, where he was hired after completing an intensive twelve-month course in fashion at the Institut Français de la Mode in Paris. At Givenchy, he worked first with Julien Macdonald, and then, after Macdonald's departure, with creative director Riccardo Tisci. Henry worked closely with Tisci for three years, but left in 2009 because he "missed meeting the client and creating everyday wardrobe pieces." From Givenchy, he worked at Paula Ka, where he took pleasure in creating pieces for women that he could relate to. Then, in 2009, he received the call from Carven. After just one season under Henry's direction, the label's distribution more than doubled. In March of 2010, Natalie Massenet of Net-A-Porter hosted a dinner to introduce Carven to the London press and at the event she compared Henry to a "young Yves Saint Laurent."

For Spring 2010, Henry's third collection for Carven, he described the overall look as "bourgeois, but with a nasty side." The shapes were simple—sleeveless shifts and full-skirted cocktail dresses—but with clever, edgy elements such as removable collars or cutaway bodices. He followed up with an equally successful collection for the following fall, pairing chic little black dresses with cropped sweaters and wool miniskirts with shrunken jackets. The youthful, suggestive elements were still perfectly in place, such as the nude lace detailing under the bust of a proper tartan shift or the red skirt suit that

was paired with just a bra. The style on the whole, however, was proper, with a look he called *bonne manière*, "to be properly dressed; I can't fight what I like."

For Spring 2012, Henry brought back Carven menswear, a line that he described as the younger brother of the Carven girl. The collection was inspired by childhood schoolboy clothing including pleated shorts, Peter Pan collars, and cropped pants. As was often the case with his women's collections, the line was proper and well-mannered.

He kept his vision in place for Fall 2012, a collection inspired by Hieronymus Bosch's *Garden of Earthly Delights*. The famous Dutch painting served as the reference for a colorful print, while a Renaissance portrait of the Madonna inspired the wings on a cocktail dress and a stained-glass-window print. The religious references were subverted by mid thigh hemlines, laser-cut skirts, and slits on bodices that revealed just the right amount of skin.

References aside, the Carven girl is fun and feminine with a proper, slightly bookish side. She "will always be in between childhood and adulthood," said Henry of his muse. And the formula seems to be working. Within just a few short years, Guillaume Henry has taken Carven out of obscurity and catapulted the line to the forefront of Paris fashion.

1978 Born in France on December 18
2001 After studying at the Ecole de Beaux Arts de Troyes and the Ecole Supérieure d'Arts Appliques Duperré (Fashion Design) in Paris, graduates from twelve-month course at the Institut Français de la Mode and interns with Givenchy and Peclers
2003 Interns as women's ready-to-wear designer at Givenchy
2005 Named senior designer at Givenchy alongside Riccardo Tisci
2006–09 Designs for Paule Ka
2009 Appointed creative director of Carven, which he relaunches as a ready-to-wear label
2012 Reintroduces Carven menswear

Guillaume Henry of Carven, 2011

1945 Founding of French luxury house
Céline by Céline Vipiana

1962 Premiere of the first
James Bond film, *Dr. No*

1953 Decoding of the structure of
deoxyribonucleic acid (DNA)

1967 David Hockney paints
A Bigger Splash

1977 Jimmy Carter
sworn in as 39th
US president

1930   1935   1940   1945   1950   1955   1960   1965   1970   1975   1980

Phoebe Philo for Celine Spring/Summer 2011
Prêt-à-Porter collection, Paris

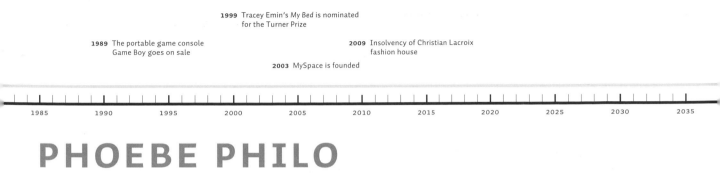

1999 Tracey Emin's *My Bed* is nominated
for the Turner Prize

1989 The portable game console
Game Boy goes on sale

2009 Insolvency of Christian Lacroix
fashion house

2003 MySpace is founded

1985   1990   1995   2000   2005   2010   2015   2020   2025   2030   2035

PHOEBE PHILO

The fashion world has watched Phoebe Philo grow up. From the free-spirited, girlish designs that invigorated Chloé to the clean, sophisticated lines that have reinvented Celine, Philo designs clothes that she herself would want to wear.

It's fitting then, that the youthful, thrown-together aesthetic that made Chloé a success was designed by a chic London-based twentysomething and the polished, urban uniforms of Celine by her grown-up, married-with-children self.

Born in Paris in 1973 to British parents, Phoebe Philo's family moved back to Britain two years later, settling in Harrow, a suburban section of northwest London. Her mother, a graphic designer with a love of fashion, fostered her daughter's interest in design, buying her a sewing machine in high school and recounting how, at age ten, Philo altered her school leotard to resemble Madonna's. Philo matriculated at Central Saint Martins where she studied design, finding herself pulled towards the styles of Helmut Lang and Jil Sander, designers with edgy, minimalist tendencies. A year after graduation, in 1997, Philo went to work with her friend Stella McCartney, who had just been named the creative director of Chloé. Four years later, when McCartney left to start her own line, Philo was named her successor. Often credited as the one who made Chloé "cool," Philo was responsible for creating some of the early twenty first century's key pieces. Her high-waisted jeans and floaty mini-dresses defined a look of the time and her infamous Paddington bag, with its short straps and big buckle, was seen on more than a few famous arms. For five years Philo grew the brand, and then, suddenly, at the height of her success, she resigned. The reason was simple: she wanted to spend time with her family, which included art-dealer husband Max Wigram and their new baby girl, Maya. Philo spent the next three years with her children (she gave birth to a son named Marlowe in 2006).

Then, in 2008, came the opportunity of a lifetime when the French luxury company, LVMH, offered Philo the creative director position at Celine, a "clean slate," as Philo referred to it. With her debut at Celine, for the 2010 resort season, Phoebe Philo's Chloé girl grew up. The look was sophisticated and polished, but not without signature Philo elements, such as a neutral palette and subtle design details. When her spring collection for the same year showed, the designer was met with raves. She had, once again, tapped the source of what every thirty-something woman wanted to wear. Her clean lines and contemporary minimalism took their form in fluid, high-waisted trousers and updated military jackets. Within months, Celine sales soared. It was official: Phoebe Philo was back. Her clothes were no-fuss—just fashion essentials for a chic brand of modern woman. The designs, in her words, were "Strong. Powerful. Reduced," clothes for grown-up women that referenced Helmut Lang's confident sexuality.

And once again, Philo struck gold with handbags: this time with her structured two-handle tote. The simple, unadorned bag was a perfect addition to Celine's signature sparseness, and so agreed the countless fashion editors and style-obsessed woman who bought it. "I felt it was time for a more back-to-reality approach to fashion," Philo said to Mark Holgate in a 2010 *Vogue* article.

For Fall 2011, Philo took the idea of driving one step further, with a collection inspired by luxury automobiles—pants with leather stripes down the side, car-wash pleat skirts, and chevron-printed sweatshirts. Philo's coats, too, referenced the subtle theme, with interior straps that fastened around the waist like seatbelts. Unlike many of her contemporaries, Philo doesn't favor trends over classic style, which is, perhaps, exactly what has made Celine a favorite over the past few years. The company's sales have proved just that, as have the empty racks at the Celine boutique in Paris, where collection after collection and bag after bag repeatedly sells out. Philo's influence at Celine is far reaching even after just a few years, with countless industry accolades and ever-growing sales; but all that aside, you know you've really made it when Kanye West puts your name in a song.

1973 Born in Paris
1993–96 Degree in fashion design at Central Saint Martins
1997 Moves to Paris to be Stella McCartney's first assistant at Chloé
2001–06 Creative director at Chloé
2004 Wins British Designer of the Year award
2008 Becomes creative director at Celine
2010 Named Designer of the Year at British Fashion Awards

Phoebe Philo, 2010

| 1930 | 1935 | 1940 | 1945 | 1950 | 1955 | 1960 | 1965 | 1970 | 1975 | 1980 |

Richard Chai Spring 2012 show,
Mercedes-Benz Fashion Week, New York

1983 Production of first commercial mobile phone　　**1994** First issue of Vice magazine is published　　**2008** Lady Gaga releases her debut album *The Fame*

2005 Founding of YouTube

1985　1990　1995　2000　2005　2010　2015　2020　2025　2030　2035

RICHARD CHAI

The ability to design classic sportswear pieces that walk the line between masculine and feminine is a skill that Richard Chai has been honing since he was a teenager. The designer's sophisticated, yet minimal, aesthetic carries through each season, while also maintaining a youthful elegance rooted in streetwear.

Born in 1974 in New Jersey, Chai signed up for evening classes in graphic design at Parson School of Design at age thirteen. While there, he caught a glimpse of a fashion drawing session that instantly impacted. "I knew then and there I wanted to be a designer. It was intoxicating," he said. And so it began. Years later, he enrolled at Parsons for school and while studying there he interned at Geoffrey Beene, working under Alber Elbaz, as well as stints at Oscar de la Renta and Christian Dior. Upon graduation, Chai continued his studies at the Institut Supérieur des Arts Appliqués in Paris and sketched for Lanvin, where Elbaz had become the creative director. In 1997, he returned to New York as an assistant designer at Armani Exchange and then moved to work on the creative team at DKNY. The following year, the young designer was appointed the design director of both the Marc Jacobs men's and women's collections and in 2001 he launched the men's Marc by Marc Jacobs line. He left Marc Jacobs shortly thereafter, becoming the creative design director of TSE and tsesay, where he worked for two years.

In 2003, after several of his TSE pieces were worn by Oprah, Jennifer Lopez, and cast members of *Sex and the City*, Chai decided to launch his own line. His debut was at New York Fashion Week in September 2004, with a front row filled with buyers from Saks Fifth Avenue, Bergdorf Goodman, and Barneys. The muted palette of his Spring 2005 collection played with subtle textures, mixing crisp fabrics with softer elements, while the shapes remained tailored and fitted. The look was cool and modern with a minimalist aesthetic, a refreshing, wearable look for urban young women.

In 2008, Chai presented a stellar fall collection after months of consultation and branding with art director, Fabien Baron. The collection was Chai's most impressive show to date, incorporating his seamless blending of masculine elements such as biker jackets and slouchy pants with sexy, feminine pieces like chiffon dresses. His knits came in autumnal shades like rich chocolate brown and forest green. Chai's use of texture was also strong, with layered looks that incorporated cropped shearling jackets, sequined waistcoats, and slim, perfectly slouched pants in subtle brocade. When Chai said "I feel like I have a new confidence within myself. This is my vision," the fashion critics all agreed.

In 2009, at the height of the world financial crisis, Chai wisely chose to launch a new, lower-priced line, Richard Chai Love, which he ended up showing on the runway instead for the Spring 2010 season. He described the new collection as the "girl-friend" to his new contemporary menswear line, which he had launched in June 2008. Love remained closely in tune with the designer collection, focusing more on individual pieces and drawing from a slightly sportier look. The designer's signature mix of masculine and feminine remained, with tailored blazers, rumpled loose-fitting pants, and slouchy, printed dresses.

For Fall 2012, Chai announced his goal for the show was to be "clean and crisp, accessible and believable," which he achieved by playing with feminine takes on classic menswear. The collection was inspired by a photograph of a man wearing a chesterfield coat taken by Bruce Davidson, and the striped tweeds and the waist-defining details came together for a polished, slightly woodsy, effect.

Richard Chai's signature boy-meets-girl aesthetic is infused with a classic sensibility and an appreciation of classic American sportswear. The designer put it best when he said "[It's] quite understated, sophisticated and elegant. Yet at the same time it has a downtown edge."

1974 Born in New York City
1987 Begins studying fashion illustration at Parsons School of Design
1996 After graduating from Parsons, studies at L'Institut Supérieur des Arts Appliqués (LISSA) in Paris and sketches for Lanvin
1997 Works as assistant designer at Armani Exchange
1998–2001 Design director of Marc Jacobs men's and women's collections
2001 Launches Marc by Marc Jacobs men's line
2001–03 Creative design director of all TSE labels
2004 Richard Chai collection debuts at New York Fashion Week
2007 Becomes a member of the CFDA
2008 Launches menswear collection in Paris; designs capsule collection for Target/GO International
2009 Richard Chai begins showing his new lower-priced line, Richard Chai Love
2012 Chai becomes the creative director of Filson

Richard Chai, 2011

1946 Founding of Estée Lauder Companies in New York

1957 Soviet *Sputnik* launched

1975 British punk band The Sex Pistols forms

1969 Woodstock Festival

| 1930 | 1935 | 1940 | 1945 | 1950 | 1955 | 1960 | 1965 | 1970 | 1975 | 1980 |

Rachel Comey Fall 2006 collection, Olympus Fashion Week, New York

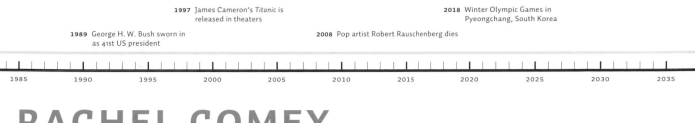
RACHEL COMEY

With roots in the New York art and music scene, Rachel Comey launched her self-titled fashion label first as a menswear line in 2001. Her introduction of womenswear began two years later, when she noticed that women were buying the cool men's tailored shirts and trousers in smaller sizes.

The former Theory designer was born and raised in Manchester, Connecticut. Comey later graduated from the University of Vermont with a degree in art and moved to New York to pursue sculpture. Once in Manhattan, Comey transitioned into costume and set design, collaborating with the punk cabaret group Gogol Bordello, helping the band to land a spot performing in the 2001 Whitney Biennial. The foray into costumes encouraged and prompted Comey to launch her menswear line, a collection of pieces partially inspired by the New York rocker scene.

Shortly thereafter, Barneys ordered several Rachel Comey pieces and then, in a moment of good fortune, David Bowie, the ultimate rock legend, wore one of the designer's shirts on the *Late Show with David Letterman*. Comey began gradually introducing a womenswear collection, officially debuting it in her Spring 2004 runway show. The women's looks, which Comey described as "airy, light, and daytime" were shown alongside her sporty menswear.

For the Fall 2008 collection, Rachel Comey staged her show at the appropriately retro Salmagundi Art Club in New York, where viewers sat on mismatched chairs in the landmark building. The quirky, forties-inspired collection was the start of Comey's now signature print-heavy look. The season was influenced by a Houdini biography, said the designer of her thirty-one piece collection. Mismatched prints found their way onto knee-length skirts and long-sleeve blouses, which when combined with textures such as alpaca and quilting, made for a charming display. With head wraps and little white ankle socks, the collection had a *Grey Gardens* feel, quirky and a bit madcap, but the individual pieces were cool and wearable.

Once she began designing womenswear, her men's collection dissolved, becoming instead just a small line of footwear and accessories. "There's just so much more to explore with women's clothes," said Comey, "there aren't as many rules and there's more room to experiment." Clothing aside, Rachel Comey's well-crafted footwear, for both men and women, has become a major part of her brand. The women's shoes often reference classic menswear styles, such as oxfords or loafers, but with feminine, sometimes quirky details that set them apart. Her wooden heel and leather ankle boots have become signatures of the footwear line and a fixture on the feet of well-dressed downtown girls.

For her Fall 2011 collection, Comey's prints once again took center stage, this time focusing on a series of graphic angles and softer abstractions. Those, along with some bright, feminine florals, were paired with oversized menswear-inspired jackets and a range of knits. For fall, the designer also introduced two new shoe designs: a low-heeled cowboy boot and a more towering stiletto shape.

For the following spring, Comey opened her show with a blousy white dress, imprinted with a landscape by the French artist Rosemarie Auberson. Of her prints for the Spring 2012 season the designer said that she was "taking them to a more subtle, textural level." This subtlety was introduced in clever ways—Comey photographed cable knit and enlarged the image, using the print on pieces such as a white and gray off-the-shoulder dress with floating chiffon sleeves and a sheer green top. There were sexier moments as well, such as a formfitting black dress with asymmetric panels of netting at the bodice and on the hem and a black-and-white print one-shoulder dress with an opening that hit high on the upper thigh, revealing more leg as the model moved.

In these intelligent plays on texture and print, Rachel Comey finds her place as one of New York's most beloved designers. Her charming, slightly off-kilter aesthetic is always evident, but as Comey develops her label, she seems more at ease with a sexier, sophisticated look. This combination, plus her line of cult-status footwear, have earned Rachel Comey a loyal fashion following.

1973 Born in Hartford, Connecticut
1994 Graduates from the University of Vermont where she studies sculpture
2001 Launches self-titled menswear line
2002 Comey's work for Gogol Bordello featured in the Whitney Biennial
2003 Debuts her womenswear collection at New York Fashion Week
2012 Launches an e-commerce site

Rachel Comey, 2009

1940 The first McDonald's
restaurant opens

1953 Hubert de Givenchy meets
Audrey Hepburn

1960 The Beatles form

1974 Beverly Johnson appears
as the first black model
on the cover of American
Vogue

1975 Microsoft is founded
in Albuquerque,
New Mexico

1930   1935   1940   1945   1950   1955   1960   1965   1970   1975   1980

Mandy Coon Fall/Winter 2012/13 collection

MANDY COON

Mandy Coon was born and raised in the suburbs outside of Houston, Texas, far from the fashion hub of New York City. Throughout her childhood, fashion meant family trips to local thrift stores and the images she saw while flipping through the pages of her mother's fashion magazines.

It wasn't until Coon was approached by a model scout at a local mall that her interest in fashion really began. Modeling became Coon's ticket out of Houston and, at age twenty, she moved to New York. Her modeling career led her to other sectors of the industry—she started working as a casting director, eventually starting her own small casting agency. Then in 2006 she headed to the Fashion Institute of Technology, where she studied haute-couture sewing and tailoring along with pattern making, learning the specialized techniques of her craft. It was while studying at FIT that the young designer realized her love of design and her desire to combine precise, meticulous details with functionality.

After school, Coon became Camilla Stærk's assistant, working as an apprentice for the designer from 2008 to 2010. Employing the skills she'd learned in school, Coon began crafting intricate, handmade runway pieces for Stærk's eponymous line, proving her eye for design and her extreme, precise skill. After several seasons working closely with Stærk, the designer encouraged Coon to go out on her own. For Spring 2010, Mandy Coon launched her own line, a mix of geometric pieces and easy, fluid versatility. From sporty, cocoon-shaped anoraks to asymmetric, pleated cocktail dresses, Coon's line showed true innovation. Her dark yet often whimsical aesthetic made the fashion world take note: Mandy Coon was a young designer to watch.

Just one year after her launch, Coon staged a full presentation at New York Fashion Week for her Spring 2011 collection. Her vivid prints and asymmetric shapes carried through the twenty-five looks, along with a heavy dose of her signature black. She infused the darkness with several shots of color—a bright, almost electric orange—that found its way onto a Grecian gown and a short, kimono-style romper. For this collection, Coon was influenced by jellyfish, evidenced by a very lifelike print of the sea creature, as well as leather tubing and unfinished hems that floated like tentacles. Coon's use of fabric combinations was also unexpected—burlap mixed with leather mixed with chiffon. On one chiffon-backed white leather blazer, Coon added a row of fringe inside so that when worn, it could be seen moving through the fabric. These special details, along with her fresh fabric pairings, garnered Coon's spring collection a host of great reviews.

For Mandy Coon, inspiration "could come from anywhere … art, music, film, people, movies, a lot of animals and biology." Following her sea-inspired collection, Coon found her muse in crystal formations as well as the work of David Altmejd. Altmejd's otherworldly mixed-media sculptures inspired Coon's tough leather pieces that were paired with softer panels of pleated chiffon. One of Coon's favorites from the Spring 2012 collection was a more classically feminine blue silk dress. The fitted, cap-sleeve dress featured delicately pleated side panels on the skirt and was named "Forces At Work." The special names, which Coon gives to all of her garments, are like titles of songs, evoking meaning and giving each piece its own identity. A padded silk charmeuse jacket with silk chiffon-covered chain "ribs" from the Fall 2010 collection, for instance, was coined "Night Flight to Venus," and a tiger-print silk chiffon dress from her first collection was called the "Mad Eyed Screamer." Perhaps the names come, in part, as an homage to music. Before her collection launched, Coon was known in fashion circles as one half of the DJ duo 2 Mandy DJs, playing at countless stylish clubs and parties.

Her inventive edginess and her impressive technical skill have made Mandy Coon a fashion favorite in just a few short years. Season after season her collections grow and her voice in the industry becomes stronger, proving that Mandy Coon is a true creative visionary.

1976 Born in Texas
2006 Moves to New York to study at the Fashion Institute of Technology
2008 Apprentices for Camilla Stærk
2009 Launches her own label for Spring 2010
2011 Wins the Ecco Domani Fashion Foundation Award and shows for the first time at Lincoln Center

Mandy Coon

1945 Marilyn Monroe discovered
as a photo model

1958 Truman Capote publishes his
novel *Breakfast at Tiffany's*

1969 Stonewall Uprising on
Christopher Street in New York

1976 Apple Computers
founded

1930　1935　1940　1945　1950　1955　1960　1965　1970　1975　1980

Creatures of the Wind, Fall/Winter 2012/13
collection

1989 First electronic dance music festival
Love Parade in Berlin

1986 Marc Jacobs presents his
first collection

1999 First e-book reader

2018 Winter Olympic Games
in Sochi, Russia

2011 Royal Wedding of Prince William of
Wales and Catherine Middleton

1985   1990   1995   2000   2005   2010   2015   2020   2025   2030   2035

CREATURES OF THE WIND

They hail from Chicago and they named their line after a Johnny Mathis song, but Shane Gabier and Chris Peters have, in a just a few short seasons, made Creatures of the Wind a strong presence on the New York fashion scene.

The pair met at the School of the Art Institute of Chicago where Peters was a student and Gabier a professor. Shortly after Peters graduated, the two began dating and almost immediately began working together. For their first collection, the duo did everything themselves, from making the patterns to sewing the garments. It was that launch collection that soon thereafter wound up on the cover of *Women's Wear Daily*.

After that initial boost, everything moved quickly for the pair, who still live and work together in Chicago, coming to New York frequently for meetings, production, and fashion shows. They are now, after just a few years in business, stocked at several major retailers, including Ikram in Chicago and Dover Street Market in London, and online at Net-A-Porter. In 2011, the industry at large took note when Creatures of the Wind was named a runner-up for the CFDA/Vogue Fashion Fund.

The name Creatures of the Wind comes from a song, as does each collection that Gabier and Peters design. For the Spring 2011 collection, their musical focal point was "The End of the World" by Skeeter Davis, and then for the following fall, "The Song of the Siren." The process, they've said, is "about creating a dialogue with the song to create a feeling." For Fall 2011, Gabier and Peters drew inspiration, as well, from a trip to Nantucket that started them thinking about sailors' wives and the "romanticism of waiting for a husband they don't know for sure is coming back." The eighteen-look collection received accolades and the garments' copious special details, such as lace handmade in Calais, France, did not go unnoticed. The collection featured a mix of color and texture, including a mohair tartan jacket and a fitted tweed skirt in bright, almost electric, blue-green.

Their Spring 2012 collection grew out of some very different references—"psychedelics, late-sixties mystics" were the buzzwords for the season. The psychedelia manifested itself in the form of floral jacquard, acid green, electric pink, and one long, tie-dyed deep-purple dress. The collection was not head-to-toe color, however; included were two very chic little black dresses and a noteworthy white sheath dress with sequined short sleeves. The extraordinary details and expert technique were, once again, an important feature of the collection. The Creatures of the Wind designers take much pride in their production, working with couture mills and using really beautiful fabrics.

Gabier and Peters are more than just fashion designers—they are true dreamers. They refuse to compromise their high-end production or their unique vision. For Fall 2012, they showed an almost couture-level collection inspired by *The Secret Commonwealth of Elves, Fauns, and Fairies*. The book, a seventeenth-century collection of tales about the supernatural, lent the collection a dreamy, often otherworldly feeling. The finale look, for instance, was a whimsical mint-green gown with tiers made from twenty-five yards of chiffon. The dreamy confection of a dress was made not without challenge, said Gabier. "We've done a lot of overlays and combinations of garments, but there's never been so much actual fabric!" The fall show took place in the Desmond Tutu Center, a Gothic, cavernous hall that transported visitors to a different time and place. "We always like to frame it with a bit of atmosphere," Gabier explained of the choice. They nicely bridged the divide between fantasy and reality, making intricate clothes that would also work perfectly in the real world and in the real closets of women. Their formula, a mix of magic and expert construction, has made Creatures of the Wind one of New York's most enchanting new lines.

2007 Shane Gabier and Christopher Peters found Creatures of the Wind
2009 Collaborate with artist Stephen Eichhorn
2010 New York Fashion Week
2011 Named a runner-up for the CFDA/Vogue Fashion Fund
2012 Creatures of the Wind design a collection for J. Crew

Shane Gabier and Chris Peters of Creatures of the Wind

Creatures of the Wind, Spring/Summer
2012 collection

Creatures of the Wind, Spring/Summer
2012 collection

1949 Premiere of Arthur Miller's
play *Death of a Salesman*

1962 Andy Warhol's first New York solo
Pop Art exhibition at Stable Gallery

1976 Founding of
The Body Shop

1955 *The Family of Man* exhibition at the
Museum of Modern Art in New York

| 1930 | 1935 | 1940 | 1945 | 1950 | 1955 | 1960 | 1965 | 1970 | 1975 | 1980 |

Cushnie et Ochs Fall/Winter 2012/13 collection

1985 Donna Karan presents
her first collection

2007 The final book of the *Harry Potter*
series is released

1983 Production of first commercial
mobile phone

1996 First cloned mammal
(Dolly the Sheep)

2010 World Expo in Shanghai

1985   1990   1995   2000   2005   2010   2015   2020   2025   2030   2035

CUSHNIE ET OCHS

The designers behind Cushnie et Ochs, Carly Cushnie and Michelle Ochs, have made a strong impression on fashion in a short period of time, their razor-sharp designs giving new meaning to a sexy, minimalist aesthetic.

Cushnie and Ochs joined forces in 2008 while they were both attending Parsons School of Design in New York. Since their launch collection, for Spring 2009, the label has been featured in several international publications and is stocked at some of the leading boutiques worldwide. Cushnie was born in London and attended Parsons in both Paris and New York, with internships at Donna Karan, Proenza Schouler, and Oscar de la Renta. Ochs, alternately, was raised in Maryland and while in design school interned at Marc Jacobs, Isaac Mizrahi, and Chado Ralph Rucci. Both Cushnie and Ochs graduated from Parsons in 2008 and began work right away on their new line. Their twenty-four piece launch collection included several body-conscious dresses in classic black and white, along with pale beige and hot pink. There were separates, as well, including several twists on the classic white shirt plus wide-leg trousers and leather leggings. The designs were sleek and minimal, with sexy details such as cutouts just below the bust and cropped, belly-baring tops. The palette was inspired by the gritty photography of Wolfgang Tillmans, while "the films *American Psycho* and *Face/Off* largely inspired the precision-cut minidresses, the geometric cutout lines, and the sleek racer-backs."

Their lean, pared-down aesthetic continued for the following fall. Inspired by ideas of mass production, the designers focused on a quiet palette of black and pearl gray with a few choice pieces in rust and one metallic jacket in a soft bronze. They introduced prints for their sophomore collection, including a light gray marble print that was used on minidresses and a pair of skintight pants. While simplicity and minimalism dominated, Cushnie et Ochs added in several design details, such as the pale gray dress with one sequined arm.

Cushnie et Ochs continued their body-conscious silhouette for Spring 2010. "We wanted the pieces to look poured onto the body," said Cushnie of the collection. Minidresses with revealing cutouts and sheer panels were shown as well as the smallest of short shorts and blazers. It was for Fall 2010 that the designers began to loosen their shape, if only slightly. For that season, Cushnie et Ochs mixed their signature black with chocolate brown and taupe. The show was primarily dresses, but their separates, which focused heavily on texture, displayed impressive technical skill and craftsmanship. They used ponyskin and mesh, which added richness to their already well-constructed pieces.

For Fall 2011, the designers referenced "a sexy vagabond," inspired by a road trip to Las Vegas. Their lookbook featured models, with feathers in their hair, posing on a wintry beach, along with dresses from the collection hanging on crosses. For the following season, Spring 2012, their mood board contained images of Barbie, *Mad Men's* Betty Draper, and the color pink, perhaps signifying a turn away from the darkness. The feminine lightness was undercut with a darker twist, however. In their chosen images Barbie had aged considerably and the *Mad Men* leading lady was holding a shotgun. As for pink, the color did appear for the first time at Cushnie et Ochs. Dresses came in bubblegum and canary yellow, along with several looks in their now signature black and white. They continued exploring color for Fall 2012, as well, including a series of chromatic dresses in navy, cobalt blue, and teal.

In 2009, Cushnie et Ochs received the Ecco Domani Fashion Foundation Award and two years later they were finalists for the 2011 CFDA/Vogue Fashion Fund Award. Recognition for their young label is evident, with starlets including Reese Witherspoon and Lake Bell wearing their designs on the red carpet. Carly Cushnie and Michelle Ochs' have created a label for the strong, confident woman, with designs that emphasize the female form while staying true to a minimal silhouette.

2007 Runner up and winner of Designer of the Year award at Parsons School of Design in their graduation year; their senior collections are featured in a cover story for WWD

2008 Form Cushnie et Ochs

2009 First runway show; Spring 2009 collection sold exclusively to Bergdorf Goodman

2009 Win the Ecco Domani Fashion Foundation Award

2010 Finalists for the Fashion Group International Rising Star Award

Carly Cushnie and Michelle Ochs
of Cushnie et Ochs

1943 First French "fashion week" is held

1958 Truman Capote publishes his
novel *Breakfast at Tiffany's*

1967 David Hockney paints
A Bigger Splash

1975 British punk band
The Sex Pistols forms

1977 Centre Georges
Pompidou
opens in Paris

| 1930 | 1935 | 1940 | 1945 | 1950 | 1955 | 1960 | 1965 | 1970 | 1975 | 1980 |

Julien David Fall/Winter
2012/13 collection

2003 Jean Paul Gaultier becomes creative
director of Hermès

1998 Google is founded

2008 Tom Ford directs the film
A Single Man

1988 The exhibition *Freeze* in London leads to the
breakthrough of the Young British Artists

1985 · 1990 · 1995 · 2000 · 2005 · 2010 · 2015 · 2020 · 2025 · 2030 · 2035

JULIEN DAVID

What began as a line of silk scarves in 2008 blossomed into a full womenswear label for Julien David's Spring 2011 collection. The French designer was born in Paris in 1978, but left Europe at age nineteen to study at Parsons School of Design in New York.

While in school, he worked for Narciso Rodriguez, becoming his design assistant upon graduation. David stayed with Rodriguez for three years, leaving to become the head designer for Ralph Lauren's Purple Label collection. Then, in 2006, the young designer moved to Tokyo, where he founded his own company, a label he described as "high-end goods with pop and street undercurrent."

His debut on the runway was in Paris, in March 2011, where he showed a masculine-inspired collection of twenty-two looks. The pieces were primarily black, with the pops of color coming from David's brightly colored, printed scarves. One of the collection's major strengths was its outerwear, specifically the coats, which had flared silhouettes and a flattering drop waist. David had experimented with volume in his outerwear for the first collection, as well, having his pieces custom made in Japan from a heavy, sumptuous tweed. "Jackets and outerwear are always part of my collections, I really enjoy working on these every season," the designer explained. To accompany his looks for Fall 2011, David sent each model down the runway in a mask printed with a pixilated version of her face. "I wanted to show a different perception of what a chic lady is," he said. "We did this for transformation and confusion." The decision was reminiscent of visual concepts employed by Rei Kawakubo and Junya Watanabe, two of Tokyo's most important designers.

Tokyo's rich design history has played a large part in Julien David's aesthetic, but so has the contemporary situation of the city. Just after he showed Fall 2011, a powerful earthquake and tsunami struck Japan, devastating whole areas, causing thousands of deaths. The disaster led David to ponder the end of the universe, resulting in a collection for Spring 2012 that while seemingly seasonal and inspired by streetwear, had been born out of thoughts of the "big crunch." David's signature boyish elements were firmly in place, realized as fitted tweed jackets

and little gingham shirts. But, more overt were the designer's references to the street. Baggy shorts with a blue camouflage print, oversized anoraks, and intricate teardrop tattoo prints mixed with sugary pinks and georgette blouses in a thoughtful and fresh approach to streetwear style. David's Spring 2012 collection also included two very feminine evening dresses with simple cap sleeves and full, knee-length skirts that sat over layers and layers of stiff tulle, their princess-inspired shapes offset by quirky geometric patterns and swirling teardrop designs.

Julien David's Fall 2012 collection was inspired by the outdoors and cities, the season's feminine shapes infused with sporty elements such as hoods, elastic waists, and headbands. The cool streetwear styles, when paired with David's luxurious, custom-made fabrics, took on a whole new elegance. His inspiration came across with patterns of cityscapes, in particular one white shirt dress that was printed with views of both the mountainous countryside and of the city skyline, each obscured by a shutter-like pattern.

When David says that his clothes are for "people who like well-made and playful things" its easy to see what he means. Before a collection, the designer spends months developing his custom fabrics with a mill in Ichinomiya, Japan, and then, using his inventive tailoring techniques, creates his original pieces for the label. Julien David is only a few seasons in, but his signature look of stylish streetwear has made him a designer to watch.

1978 Born in Paris
1997 Moves to New York to attend Parsons School of Design; works for Narciso Rodriguez
2003 Graduates from Parsons
2006 Moves to Tokyo where he begins freelancing
2007 Founds his own company in Japan
2011 Launches womenswear collection in Paris
2012 Finalist for ANDAM Fashion Award

Julien David

1966 Italian luxury goods house
Bottega Veneta is founded

1942 Peggy Guggenheim opens her Art of
this Century Gallery in New York

1959 First Barbie doll show at toy
fair in New York

1971 MoMA PS1 is established

1956 Elvis Presley releases
"Heartbreak Hotel," his first big hit

1973 First commercial PC

1930   1935   1940   1945   1950   1955   1960   1965   1970   1975   1980

Giles Deacon Spring 2012 collection,
Lunch with Margaret and George Event,
Toronto

1995 Launch of the Japanese electronic
    toy Tamagotchi

2009 Insolvency of Christian Lacroix
    fashion house

1988 Anna Wintour becomes editor-in-chief
    of American *Vogue*

| 1985 | 1990 | 1995 | 2000 | 2005 | 2010 | 2015 | 2020 | 2025 | 2030 | 2035 |

GILES DEACON

Born in 1969 in the small town of Darlington in northeast England, Giles Deacon's designs are the perfect mix of quirk and luxury, all crafted with a highly skilled hand.

Deacon moved from his hometown to London in 1988 to attend Central Saint Martins, from which he graduated with a degree in design, along with class-mates Alexander McQueen, Luella Bartley, and stylist Katie Grand, who he dated after school. Upon graduation, Deacon contributed illustrations to Grand's magazine, *Dazed & Confused*, and began designing a line called Doran Deacon with his friend Fi Doran. Soon after, Deacon moved to Paris to work for Jean-Charles de Castelbajac. In 1998, Grand introduced the young designer to the owner of Bottega Veneta, who promptly hired him as the chief designer, where he worked for three seasons before landing at Gucci. In 2003 he left Gucci and estab-lished his own line, Giles, setting up a communal studio in a Victorian schoolhouse in London.

The year 2004 marked Giles' debut on the run-way during London Fashion Week. The show was styled by then ex-girlfriend Katie Grand and worn by models including Linda Evangelista, Eva Herzigova, and Karen Elson. The thirty-four-year-old's first collection of nipped-waist suits, pencil skirts, and wide-shouldered jackets came in an exciting range of materials—custom prints of trippy wooded scenes, Scottish tweed, and bespoke jacquards. There were leather accessories, too, molded into the shape of beetles and worn around models' necks on selected outfits of the large, fifty-two look collection. Within the year, Deacon was named the Best New Designer at the British Fashion Awards and two years later, in 2006, he earned the Designer of the Year title.

By the end of the decade, Deacon had several collaborations under his belt, including collections for Daks, Mulberry, Converse, Smythson, and a line for high-street retailer New Look. In a 2012 interview with Canadian *Elle*, he explained that "It's impor-tant to offer well-thought-out pieces at lower prices." In 2010, Deacon was tapped to become the chief designer for Emanuel Ungaro and his debut collection showed in the fall of that year. His Spring

2011 line featured feminine pastels and feather head-dresses, whereas his follow-up for fall was tough and edgy, with black jumpsuits, corseted cocktail dresses, and leather molding.

Giles parted ways with Ungaro in 2011, showing his Spring 2012 collection just weeks after the news broke. The dreaminess of his spring show was of epic proportions, with a background of silver clouds and massive swan headpieces by Stephen Jones. The clothes themselves ranged from pink and white gowns adorned with ostrich feathers to metallic-silver cocktail dresses with laser-cut designs. Deacon's inspiration for the whimsical show began when he designed costumes for the English National Ballet's production of *Black Swan*, but he abandoned the darker side of the story in favor of "the broader world of the swan."

The Fall 2012 Giles collection retained the magic, but skewed quite a bit darker than the previous season. The inspiration for fall was disaster, albeit one straight out of a fairy tale. "I just had this idea of someone rushing out of a beautiful house," Deacon said of his vision. "It's burning down, and what are you going to take?" The trans-lation, while stately and beautiful, was also quite literal, with burns on tuxedo coats and singed dresses. The painterly prints and the elegant sil-houettes drew the viewer easily inside the imagina-tive world of Giles Deacon.

Deacon's vision is one where the past and the future meet, his collection often full of historical references but created with a forward-thinking point of view. The Giles woman, who includes Drew Barrymore, Scarlett Johansson, and others, doesn't take herself too seriously, appreciating the designer's irreverence. "We dress a cross section of twenty- to seventy-year-olds," Deacon said, "and the thing that ties them all together is that they're interested in a certain type of quality and design—it's not just about a trend."

1969 Born in Darlington, England
1988–92 Studies fashion at Central
    Saint Martins, London
1992 Contributes illustrations to
    Dazed & Confused; launches
    Doran Deacon line with Fi Doran;
    moves to Paris to work with
    Jean-Charles de Castelbajac for
    two years
1998–2001 Chief designer for
    Bottega Veneta
2001–02 Hired by Tom Ford to design
    for Gucci
2003 Founds the Giles label
2004 Debuts at London Fashion Week;
    named British Fashion Awards
    Best New Designer
2006 Collaborates with Converse;
    named British Fashion Awards
    Designer of the Year
2007 Introduces Mulberry for Giles
    capsule; debuts a collection for
    Daks
2008 Debuts collection for Fay in
    Milan; introduces menswear for
    New Look
2009 Collaborations with Smythson,
    Lee Cooper, and Selfridges;
    launches jewelry line and beach-
    wear; GQ's Designer of the Year;
    debuts in Paris
2010–11 Creative director of
    Emanuel Ungaro

Giles Deacon, 2011

1953 French actress Isabelle Huppert
is born

1947 Swedish retail-clothing company   **1960** The Beatles form   **1975** Microsoft is founded
Hennes & Mauritz is founded   in Albuquerque,
                                                                                     New Mexico

1955 First Documenta exhibition
in Kassel

| 1930 | 1935 | 1940 | 1945 | 1950 | 1955 | 1960 | 1965 | 1970 | 1975 | 1980 |

Patrik Ervell Fall 2009 Menswear show,
Mercedes-Benz Fashion Week, New York

1987 *The Bonfire of the Vanities* by
Tom Wolfe is published

1993 Bill Clinton sworn in as
42nd US president

2008 Lady Gaga releases her debut
album *The Fame*

2012 Picasso's *Nu au Plateau de Sculpteur*
fetches $106.5 million at Christie's

1985   1990   1995   2000   2005   2010   2015   2020   2025   2030   2035

PATRIK ERVELL

Patrik Ervell's particular brand of menswear is modern and stylish, without being complicated and hard to wear. The designer's blend of classic tailoring with innovative, future-thinking elements has made his label a success with both critics and customers.

Ervell was born in 1978 in San Francisco, California, the son of Swedish parents. As a child, the family lived in California, Sweden, and London, perhaps inspiring Ervell to enroll at University of California, Berkeley, with a focus in political science, economics, and international relations. In 2001, after graduating, Ervell relocated to New York with the intention of working in the State Department, but instead his focus shifted to fashion when he landed a Job as an editor at *V Magazine*, where he worked for several years. In 2005, Ervell created a small run of T-shirts for Opening Ceremony, a move that led him to design an entire collection of menswear.

By 2006, Ervell was producing a full collection, winning the Ecco Domani Award for best menswear designer that same year. His first collection, shown in September 2005, was created when Ervell was just twenty-six years old. Ervell had taken technical classes at Parsons, preparing for his first twenty-piece collection. The Spring 2006 pieces included slim suiting, trench coats, sweatshirts, and all of the other elements needed to form the perfect men's wardrobe. The young designer's goal was modernity, with a self-proclaimed disdain for clothes that were anything but, and the collection reflected just that with its technical fabrics, including a highly resistant coated nylon and a machine-made embroidery. Details were another focus of the collection, with trimmed pockets and hand-finished buttonholes that added a dose of luxury to the pieces. This attention to detail has become an Ervell signature, with the following year's fall collection featuring mother-of-pearl buttons on shirts and biker jackets with braid trimming on the pockets.

Patrik Ervell's modern, detail-oriented aesthetic continued, a look the designer described as "American sportswear without clichés." His pieces, an expert blend of modern technology and handcrafted luxury, are updated twists on the classics. For instance, a hooded rain jacket from Spring 2007 was made from semitransparent recycled parachutes that showed the seams and construction. The combination, for Ervell, is more "romantic than stark. I don't think of modern as having to be stripped bare of ornamentation," he told *New York Times Magazine*. "With men's wear, you don't have to reinvent the wheel every season ... little details, subtle messages rules you have to work in."

Ervell's aesthetic is not about reinventing the wheel, but instead the designer's vision is a wardrobe of pieces that look and feel good, inside and out. His angular clothes, which get more impressive by the season, manage to be both utilitarian and romantic. For Fall 2011, he referenced the Air Force with a backdrop of parachutes and a collection filled with bomber jackets and flight suits. Mixed in with preppy classics like button-up shirts and tweed suits were more experimental pieces, including a rubber sweatshirt and voluminous, billowing coats.

By the time Ervell showed his Fall 2012 collection, he had expanded the label to include womenswear. His men's pieces retained their signature tailoring and plays on sportswear, including formal pants with elasticized cuffs and raincoats layered over slim-fitting suits. The ten women's looks consisted of sharp suiting, silk jumpsuits, and tailored trousers, along with sportier bomber jackets and floral-print jeans. To debut the collection before the show, Ervell dressed his friend Kirsten Dunst in a slim navy wool tuxedo with hand-painted lapels.

"I want to make something more than clothes," Ervell said. "I want to send a bigger aesthetic message." The message is one of quiet luxury, a combination of beautifully crafted pieces and modern sportswear. Ervell's love of modernity translated to his sales approach as well, with the designer creating his first store online instead of opening a brick-and-mortar location. Patrik Ervell's insistence on innovation has maintained his label as a New York favorite that is never short on style or craftsmanship.

1978 Born in San Francisco
2001 Graduates from University of California, Berkeley and moves to New York where he works as an editor at *V Magazine*
2005 Creates T-shirts for Opening Ceremony
2006 Ervell begins designing a full menswear collection
2007 Wins the Ecco Domani Fashion Foundation Award and stages first runway show
2010 Launches online store
2011 Nominated for GQ's Best New Menswear Designer in America

Patrik Ervell, 2008

1946 Founding of Estée Lauder
Companies in New York

1958 Truman Capote publishes his
novel *Breakfast at Tiffany's*

1974 Malcolm McLaren and
Vivienne Westwood
open their boutique
SEX in London

1930   1935   1940   1945   1950   1955   1960   1965   1970   1975   1980

Prabal Gurung Fall 2012 show,
Mercedes-Benz Fashion Week, New York

1979 Margaret Thatcher becomes British Prime Minister

1989 The portable game console Game Boy goes on sale

1995 Damien Hirst is awarded the Turner Prize

2001 First same-sex marriage in the Netherlands

2010 The Burj Khalifa in Dubai is officially opened

1985 1990 1995 2000 2005 2010 2015 2020 2025 2030 2035

PRABAL GURUNG

Prabal Gurung creates clothes to make women look beautiful. The designer has said that his motivation is not to "chase what is cool," but to simplify the fashion process for women and to inspire beauty. Since the launch of his eponymous label in 2009, Gurung has dressed some of the world's most powerful women with just that motto in mind.

Prabal Gurung was born in 1974 in Singapore and raised in Kathmandu, Nepal. The worldly Gurung's design education began in New Delhi, where he studied at the National Institute of Fashion Technology. While in school, he apprenticed at several local fashion houses and production companies. He began designing with Manish Arora and spent time traveling to England and Australia assisting stylists with fashion shows and editorial photo shoots. In 1999, after seven years of traveling and assisting, Gurung moved to New York to attend Parsons School of Art and Design. He soon landed an internship with Donna Karan and upon graduating worked with Cynthia Rowley. He spent two years at Rowley, where he learned about both the design and business ends of the fashion industry. His training there prepared him for his next position as the design director at Bill Blass. Gurung spent five successful years at Bill Blass and in February 2009, when Blass closed, he launched his own line, Prabal Gurung.

When Gurung showed that February at New York Fashion Week, he was met with great reviews. The designer described the collection as "clothes for a thinking-man's sex symbol." There were elements of Yves Saint Laurent, one of Gurung's design inspirations, woven throughout the collection as well. The show's nineteen looks were mostly for evening, with several graphic dresses and no shortage of luxe details, such as a skirt of hand-sewn feathers. The black, white, and red collection also featured Gurung's modern take on some of YSL's classics, such as Le Smoking. At a time when the world was entering into a recession, Gurung showed a collection of dresses that retailed for over $2,000. Of the collection, the brave designer said, "I just want to do beautiful, well-made clothes."

For his sophomore collection, the designer stayed true to his words. His inspiration for the Spring 2010 line was taken from a bottle of his mother's YSL perfume from the seventies. Gurung loved the bottle and wanted to play with the idea of packaging. His expert draping technique and attention to detail stood out, proving the collection a success. Again his palette was simple—this time with bright blue in place of the previous season's red—but his one-shoulder cocktail dresses and draped gowns were anything but. Gurung's technique, his use of the finest materials, and his devotion to making beautiful clothes came together to form a chic and utterly sophisticated collection.

Celebrities and powerful women alike are drawn to Gurung's stylish designs. Michelle Obama has worn Prabal Gurung to several events, including the high-profile Governors' Dinner and a September 11 memorial concert. Gurung also counts Oprah Winfrey and Demi Moore as fans, and in January 2011 he reached a younger audience when fourteen-year-old actress Hailee Steinfeld wore one of his gowns to the Golden Globe Awards.

Since he launched in 2009, Prabal Gurung has made a name for himself designing gowns and dresses for boldfaced women. His high-fashion pieces are well made, but never avant-garde or hard to wear. Each season his inspiration is far reaching—for the Spring 2012 season he looked at erotic photographs by Nobuyoshi Araki, while the Fall 2011 collection drew reference from *Great Expectations'* Miss Havisham. Of his international success Gurung has said, "The thing I feel most proud of though is how I've managed to highlight Nepal, where I grew up. It's such a poor place and I think the little success I have has helped inspire a few of the people who live there. I get thousands of letters from them—I hope it's made them think their dreams can come true too."

1974 Born in Singapore
1999 Moves to New York to study at Parsons School of Design
2009 Leaves design position at Bill Blass to launch his womenswear label
2010 Receives the Ecco Domani Fashion Foundation Award and is a runner-up for the CFDA/Vogue Fashion Fund Award
2011 First Lady Michelle Obama wears Prabal Gurung to multiple events, including the Governors' Dinner and a 9/11 memorial concert

Prabal Gurung, 2011

1943 Premiere of *Casablanca*, directed by Michael Curtiz

1956–59 Guggenheim Museum constructed in New York

1961 Construction of the Berlin Wall

1979 Sony begins selling the Walkman

1930   1935   1940   1945   1950   1955   1960   1965   1970   1975   1980

Christopher Kane Spring/Summer 2009 collection, London Fashion Week

1999 Prada takes over the fashion houses
of Jil Sander and Helmut Lang

1995 *Toy Story* is the first wholly
computer-generated film

2009 Barack Obama sworn in
as 44th US president

981 First recognized cases of AIDS

2010 Jonathan Franzen publishes
his novel *Freedom*

1985   1990   1995   2000   2005   2010   2015   2020   2025   2030   2035

CHRISTOPHER KANE

For Christopher Kane, it all started in September 2006 with some very tiny neon bandage dresses, when the then twenty-four-year-old British designer paraded thirty-two body-hugging minidresses down the runway.

The dresses conjured up memories of Hervé Léger and Azzedine Alaïa's infamous clinging looks from the eighties and nineties. And Kane's color palette was breathtaking, with combinations of pink and red, lime green with beige, and electric fluorescent yellow with just about everything. There were crystals, ruffles, and zippers, not to mention a show's worth of shoes on loan from Versace. The footwear was thanks to Donatella Versace herself, who had showed her support for Kane since his graduation the year before.

Christopher Kane was born in 1982 in Newarthill, Scotland, the youngest of five children. He attended Central Saint Martins College of Art and Design, working with designers Giles Deacon and Russell Sage while still in school. In 2006, his graduate collection won the Harrods Design Award. Immediately following graduation, Versace hired him to work on the label's couture collection as well as consult on their shoes and accessories. That same year, Kane established his own eponymous label with his sister, Tammy, who ran the business side of the company as well as serving as the in-house model and muse. The two worked, in Kane's rented East End apartment, to create and launch the first collection for Spring 2007. Those neon dresses, which, said Kane, were intended to be "as bright as possible," made a big splash on the London fashion scene.

Critics speculated whether Kane would be able to move beyond his youthful fluorescent minis and, without question, he did. His second collection, for Fall/Winter 2007/08, delved into the darkness, with tough leather, rich velvet, and a hefty dose of black. The dark tones were mixed with lush jewel tones of burnt orange, deep red, and emerald green. Just one year out of school and the industry was swooning, some saying that Kane was "the strongest talent to have emerged in London in a decade."

Then, just a few days before his third collection was slated to show during London Fashion Week, the designer reported that twenty-three pieces had been stolen from his studio. The looks were not recovered, but, seven days later, Kane showed his Spring 2008 line. The collection was yet another departure, this time featuring a mix of western shirts, snakeskin prints, and floaty chiffon ruffles. Gone were the body-conscious shapes, replaced with romantic, western pieces and stonewashed, distressed denim. The inspiration allegedly came from late-night viewings of horror films as a child. Also in play for inspiration were the inexpensive tees that he and Tammy had been wearing to work during the summer, a camouflage print, and a loose-fitting T-shirt dress, respectively, that worked their way into the season's collection.

That same year, Kane was awarded New Designer of the Year at the British Fashion Awards and began working with musicians such as Beth Ditto and Kylie Minogue on costumes. He also partnered with Johnstons of Elgin to make a line of cashmere pieces and worked with Lancôme to create limited-edition lipgloss.

His success continued, and then, in 2009, Kane struck gold with his spring collection, which sold out on Net-A-Porter.com within twenty-four hours of launching. The dinosaur-inspired collection was filled with animal-spot sweaters in candy-colored brights and geometric, 3-D skirts that were cut to resemble scales. The collection was conceptually innovative, but still accessible and easy to wear. Later that year, Kane showed his fall collection, a hip and refreshing mix of masculine trousers, leather motorcycle jackets and feminine striped organza dresses. The stripes came from staring at a blank television screen, said the designer, and the look on the whole was "a bit of a twisted sister."

In the few short years since his label's inception, Christopher Kane has covered countless themes. From his Scottish-schoolgirls-gone-bad for Spring 2010 to the ladylike fluorescent lace of his Spring 2011 collection, Kane is one of most creative and exciting British designers today.

1982 Born in Newarthill, Scotland
2000 Moves to London to attend Central Saint Martins; works with Russell Sage and Giles Deacon
2005 Wins the Lancôme Color Design Award
2006 Graduates with a master's in womenswear from Central Saint Martins; wins Harrods Design Award; hired by Versace to work on Atelier couture collection; launches own line with his sister Tammy in East London
2007 Presents first collection; capsule collection for Topshop hits stores; named New Designer of the Year at the British Fashion Awards; designs costumes for Beth Ditto and Kylie Minogue
2008 Collaborates with Johnstons of Elgin and Lancôme
2009 Spring collection sells out in twenty-four hours on Net-A-Porter; wins the British Fashion Council's Collection of the Year award.
2010 Actresses Emma Watson, Carey Mulligan, and Diane Kruger wear his line; shows his work in Mumbai during Lakmé Fashion Week

Christopher Kane, 2011

Christopher Kane Spring/Summer 2009
collection, London Fashion Week

Christopher Kane Spring/Summer 2009
collection, London Fashion Week

1955 *The Family of Man* exhibition at the
Museum of Modern Art in New York

1949 Premiere of Arthur Miller's play
Death of a Salesman

1964 British fashion clothing retailer
Topshop is founded

1977 Centre Georges
Pompidou
opens in Paris

1930   1935   1940   1945   1950   1955   1960   1965   1970   1975   1980

Mary Katrantzou Spring/Summer 2011
collection

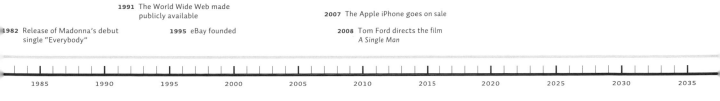

1991 The World Wide Web made publicly available

2007 The Apple iPhone goes on sale

1982 Release of Madonna's debut single "Everybody"

1995 eBay founded

2008 Tom Ford directs the film *A Single Man*

1985   1990   1995   2000   2005   2010   2015   2020   2025   2030   2035

MARY KATRANTZOU

Mary Katrantzou is quickly making a name for herself in the fashion world as a talented designer whose often couture-like pieces incorporate some of the industry's most exciting prints to date.

The Greek designer was born in 1983 in Athens to an interior designer mother and a father trained in textiles. Katrantzou first moved to America to study architecture at the Rhode Island School of Design before transferring to Central Saint Martins College in London, where she graduated with a degree in textile design. While in school, Katrantzou began selling her textile prints to Bill Blass, prompting a shift in focus from interior to fashion prints. Then, in 2006, she spent two seasons working on prints with designer Sophia Kokosalaki. Katrantzou went on to complete her Master's in Fashion at Central Saint Martins and she opened the 2008 runway show there with a collection of trompe-l'oeil digital prints on jersey dresses. The pieces, with their prints of oversized jewelry, created the illusion of wearing giant necklaces, inspired by Russian Constructivism and early-seventies movie posters. There was real jewelry as well, exact replicas of Katrantzou's prints made from wood and metal.

Katrantzou produced her first ready-to-wear collection for Fall 2008 and debuted her new line at London Fashion Week. The nine shift dresses she showed were picked up by several notable stockists, landing Katrantzou's first collection at fifteen retailers worldwide. Fall 2009 marked her first runway show, as well as a departure from what one would expect. The seventeen looks came in a variety of new silhouettes, fluted skirts and zippered pants among them. Her graphic and colorful sophomore collection focused on more simplified images of perfume bottles, with trompe-l'oeil cut glass and delicate crystal bottle tops. Katrantzou incorporated jewelry once again, layering on large necklaces made from gold chains, tubing, and mirrors. With assistance from a London printer, the Silk Bureau, along with help from her furniture-maker mother, Katrantzou created a truly impressive second collection.

By Spring 2011, there was a significant amount of buzz surrounding Katrantzou's London show, and the young designer did not disappoint. Her inspiration came not from the models featured in the photographs of Helmut Newton and Guy Bourdin, but instead from the interiors. The clothes were printed with images of incredibly detailed swimming pools, dining room tables, and window views. Her trompe l'oeil, too, was stronger than ever, with printed chandeliers that looked like necklaces and chiffon panels on skirts that doubled as window curtains. Katrantzou's conceit was perfectly executed, coming together to make an impressive and seductive spring collection. The beautiful symmetry of her patterns reinforced her brilliance as a print maker, and the wearable, flattering shapes of her dresses solidified her as a truly talented fashion designer.

For Fall 2012, Katrantzou "was looking for different silhouettes to emphasize embroidery and embellishments." Her new forms appeared as godet skirts and corseted styles that came from research on Elizabethan England. Katrantzou also played with color for her thirty-two piece collection—a yellow look was comprised of several No. 2 pencils joined together in a row, whereas a green gown was printed with images of an elaborate manicured garden. She sourced imagery from other commonplace objects, including a typewriter, a clock, and spoons, but the pieces were far from commonplace, with intricate embellishments and complex, well-made forms. The beautiful, if often complicated, patterns were often so intense that they became abstractions, a series of colorful, geometric shapes on a garment.

There is no doubt that Mary Katrantzou pushes the limits of design, positioning her creations somewhere in between wearable fashion (which they are, no question) and fine art, with prints that could easily find there way to the wall of a gallery. Her use of serial repetition and expert employment of trompe l'oeil make Katrantzou's pieces some of the most visually stimulating designs that exist in fashion today.

1983 Born in Athens
2005 Graduates with a degree in textile design from Central Saint Martins
2006 Spends two seasons designing prints with Sophia Kokosolaki
2008 Graduates with a master's in fashion textiles from Central Saint Martins; debuts her first ready-to-wear collection at London Fashion Week
2009 First runway show
2009–11 Awarded NEWGEN sponsorship
2010 Collaborates with Topshop
2011 Wins Emerging Talent–Ready-to-Wear Award at the British Fashion Awards
2012 Shortlisted for BFC/Vogue Designer Fashion Fund

Mary Katrantzou

Mary Katrantzou Fall/Winter 2012/13
collection

Mary Katrantzou Fall/Winter
2012/13 collection

1942 Edward Hopper paints *Nighthawks*

1953 Decoding of the structure of deoxyribonucleic acid (DNA)

1971 First Starbuck opens

1968 The Beatles stay at Maharishi Mahesh Yogi's ashram in Rishikesh, India

1975 Microsoft is founded in Albuquerque, New Mexico

| 1930 | 1935 | 1940 | 1945 | 1950 | 1955 | 1960 | 1965 | 1970 | 1975 | 1980 |

Jenni Kayne Spring/Summer 2009 presentation, Industria Studio, New York

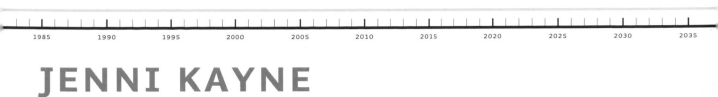
JENNI KAYNE

Jenni Kayne debuted her first collection at Los Angeles Fashion Week in 2003 when she was just nineteen years old. Born and raised in Los Angeles, Kayne had been interested in fashion from a young age, declaring at eight years old that she wanted to be a designer.

She attended the Otis College of Art and Design for a year, but left to work as a buyer for a store in Santa Monica, which allowed her to travel in Europe and learn about the industry. Her travels inspired the young designer to launch her own signature collection the following year.

Jenni Kayne's sophisticated clothes are classic, easy-to-wear pieces that are fashionable without relying on trends. "I like clothes that you can throw down on the floor and still be able to wear," said Kayne of her aesthetic to *Harper's Bazaar*. Her sportswear quickly took off, acquiring a fan base of young celebrities such as Mary-Kate and Ashley Olsen, Rachel Bilson, and Kirsten Dunst. In 2006, Jenni Kayne moved her fashion show from L.A. to New York in an effort "to be taken more seriously." Her sixteen-look New York debut for Spring 2006 was chic yet understated, with a palette of white, cream, navy, and yellow. She traded in her celebrity-filled front row (Owen Wilson, Luke Wilson, and Jared Leto had attended her last season in L.A.) for a more fashion-focused presentation that had critics praising the young designer.

Kayne's sophomore show in New York focused on outerwear, including leather trenches, long camel coats, and fitted, short-sleeve styles. Worn over cropped pants and beaded dresses, Kayne's collection covered the day-to-night pieces perfect for a modern woman's wardrobe. Her belted dresses, like a navy blue pleated chiffon look and a floor-length mustard yellow variety, were feminine, yet also completely pulled together. Kayne's brand of sophisticated cool continued, with seasonal collections that established her look of effortless American sportswear. Her eye for color also became evident, with brights and neons comfortably mixed in with classically neutral palettes.

Kayne's Spring 2011 collection was no exception. With the bicoastal inspiration of a girl who sets out on a road trip from Manhattan to Joshua Tree, Jenni Kayne's looks subtly morphed from East Coast to West. The crisp opening looks were shown in urban black and white, with leather sleeves on a black shift and paillettes on a simple white mini. By the middle of the show, however, the colors had morphed into the distinctly desert-like tones of sand, cream, and tan with a rusty orange, a soft yellow, and a bold shock of magenta providing brighter moments.

While Kayne's inspiration is always present, her themes never feel as such, providing more of a subtle reference point than an overwhelming narrative. For Spring 2012, the starting point was, in Kayne's own words, "country-club chic combined with urban athleticism," while she described the following fall as stemming from a "proper English gentleman's hunting wardrobe." She mixed in fabrics like tweed and herringbone, but not without updating them. A classic checked pattern was revamped in digitized blue, orange, and yellow, and a heavy cable knit sweater was paired with slim, electric yellow pants. She applied her understated twists to the evening looks, as well, such as the sheer floor-length black chiffon skirt that Kayne paired with a matching sheer tuxedo top.

Jenni Kayne's clothes don't claim to be more complicated or trend-driven than they are; the designer instead embraces her collection's wearable sensibility. "I think what sets the collection apart is that we offer something sophisticated and classic at a price point that's accessible to a lot of women," Kayne says. "My customer loves fashion, but she wants clothes that she'll go back to again and again." As long as she continues on her path of refined, lighthearted elegance, Jenni Kayne's customer will surely keep on returning.

1984 Born in Los Angeles
2002 Leaves Otis College of Art and Design after two semesters to work as a buyer for a store in Santa Monica; travels Europe learning the trade
2003 Debuts own line in Los Angeles at age nineteen
2005 First presentation in New York for Spring 2006
2007 Opens first store in West Hollywood
2008 Inducted into the Council of Fashion Designers of America (CFDA)

Jenni Kayne, 2009

1946 French fashion designer
Jeanne Lanvin dies

1959 Miles Davis releases the
album *Kind of Blue*

1968 Calvin Klein founds Calvin Klein
Inc. in New York

1977 First *Star Wars*
film directed
by George
Lucas

1930 — 1935 — 1940 — 1945 — 1950 — 1955 — 1960 — 1965 — 1970 — 1975 — 1980

Derek Lam Fall 2012 show,
Mercedes-Benz Fashion Week,
New York

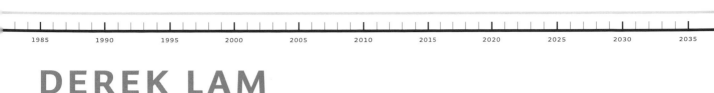

1991 US band Nirvana releases
the album *Nevermind*

2009 Barack Obama awarded
Nobel Peace Price

1997 Jean Paul Gaultier designs
futuristic costumes for Luc
Besson's film *The Fifth Element*

2012 Whitney Houston dies

1981 First issue of *i-D* magazine
is published

| 1985 | 1990 | 1995 | 2000 | 2005 | 2010 | 2015 | 2020 | 2025 | 2030 | 2035 |

DEREK LAM

By mixing Eastern and Western cultures, the East Coast and the West Coast, and city and country, Derek Lam has become one of America's most important designers. His worldly sportswear is designed with an eye to the past, but with a deep understanding of modern style.

Born in 1967 to Chinese American parents, Derek Lam was the youngest of three children to grow up in San Francisco, California. His grandparents ran a successful garment factory in San Francisco that specialized in bridal dresses and his parents imported clothing from Asia. Immersed in the garment business as a child, Lam would often spend time watching the seamstresses sew wedding gowns. It was only then that he became interested in fashion, and he attended Parsons School of Art and Design in New York. He graduated in 1990 and began working as an assistant at Michael Kors, where he spent four years under the American designer. From Kors he moved to Hong Kong to work for a large retail brand, G2000, but returned to New York in 1998 when he was named the vice president of design for Kors by Michael Kors. In 2002, after several years in that post, Lam launched his own eponymous line, working with partner and CEO Jan-Hendrik Schlottmann out of his West Village apartment.

It was Derek Lam's second collection, for Spring 2004, that caused a sensation in New York. His collection of "wildly sensuous yet oddly demure rose-print dresses" were shown at a furniture gallery in Manhattan's Meatpacking district. His clothes, which tend to focus more on femininity then formality, are an example, as the designer puts it, of "sensual, relaxed luxury." As that 2004 show revealed, Lam's references came from a place of grown-up sophistication, such as the inspiration he took from Marilyn Monroe and the film *In the Mood for Love*. The eighteen-piece show, all produced in Italy, was a success with buyers and editors alike, officially putting Derek Lam on the map. One year later, he won the CFDA Perry Ellis-Swarovski Award for Emerging Talent in Womenswear.

For his Spring 2008 show, Lam discovered his muse in photographer Guy Bourdin, who he found "young and fresh and provocative." Critics agreed that his collection, too, was just that. The leopard-print silk romper that opened the show exemplified the chic yet youthful tone of the season. The little georgette evening dresses that came in peach, gray, and pearl followed perfectly along this theme with their leg-baring hemlines and delicate seams. Paired with back-seamed black stockings, the look was polished, yet sexy.

For Spring 2012, Lam revisited his California roots, basing the collection, in part, on Robert Neutra's Kaufmann House in Palm Springs, with all of its "mid-century louche and luxury." Despite the retro reference, Lam's collection felt completely modern, with crisp white trenches, bold geometric prints, and bright pops of yellow and orange throughout. For fall of the same year, however, Lam became "thoughtful, quiet, a little more sober," inspired this time by prints from an old book he found. The show opened with several floral prints and a distinct sixties vibe, as seen in the hairdos and the silhouettes. His reinterpreted vision of the quirky sixties coed resulted in a series of beautiful cashmere knits, sexy patent pencil skirts, and luxe shearling jackets. His evening pieces, with their trailing chiffon skirts, were done in bright white and stark black. When paired with sweaters, as in the last two looks, the result was a pared-down glamour, a country elegance that would look perfectly modern for a city evening.

His blend of Eastern and Western cultures, his mix of East Coast and West Coast, and his seamless melding of city and country have proven that Derek Lam is one of America's most important designers. Lam's reinvention of contemporary sportswear is never without an addition of softer femininity or a nod to another era. His thoroughly modern sensibility has secured Lam as a fashion favorite and his worldly twists on the classics ensure that each piece he designs is special.

1967 Born in San Francisco
1985–90 Studies at Parsons School of Design; hired by Michael Kors on graduation
1998 Named VP of design for Kors by Michael Kors
2002 Launches signature line with Jan-Hendrik Schlottmann
2003 First collection debuts; wins Ecco Domani Fashion Foundation Award
2004 Nominated for CFDA Swarovski Perry Ellis Award for Womenswear; becomes a CFDA/Vogue Fashion Fund finalist
2005 Receives CFDA Swarovski Perry Ellis Award for Womenswear; debut Tod's collection shown in Paris
2006 Named creative director of Tod's; first bag collection debuts
2007 Wins CFDA Accessory Designer of the Year; starts shoe and eyewear lines
2009 Opens first boutique in New York
2011 Creates ready-to-wear line for eBay

Derek Lam, 2010

1961 Japanese fashion label Comme des
Garçons is founded by Rei Kawakubo

1949 Spanish designer
Mariano Fortuny dies

1959 First Barbie doll show at toy
fair in New York

1971 Photographer Larry Clark
publishes his book *Tulsa*

| 1930 | 1935 | 1940 | 1945 | 1950 | 1955 | 1960 | 1965 | 1970 | 1975 | 1980 |

Phillip Lim Fall 2012 show,
Mercedes-Benz Fashion Week, New York

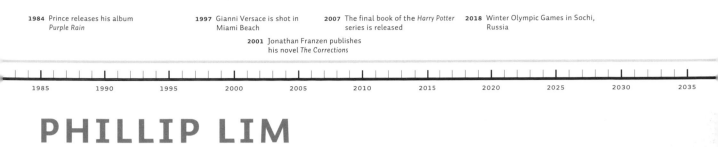

1984 Prince releases his album *Purple Rain*

1997 Gianni Versace is shot in Miami Beach

2007 The final book of the *Harry Potter* series is released

2018 Winter Olympic Games in Sochi, Russia

2001 Jonathan Franzen publishes his novel *The Corrections*

1985 1990 1995 2000 2005 2010 2015 2020 2025 2030 2035

PHILLIP LIM

The past decade has been nonstop for Phillip Lim—a series of awards, accolades, and company growth for the young designer who launched his line, 3.1 Phillip Lim, in 2004. His contemporary pieces are equally on-trend and wearable, a fashionable combination that has inspired a cult following.

Lim was born in Thailand in 1973, the youngest of six children, and the family moved to California that same year. Lim spent his childhood in Orange County, entering California State University at Long Beach in 1991 to study business and finance. His plans quickly changed and Lim, perhaps inspired by his seamstress mother, switched his focus to fashion merchandising. While in school, he worked at Barneys in Beverly Hills where one day he unpacked a box of Katayone Adeli clothes. He loved the pieces he saw and called her design studio, resulting in an internship as a design assistant. The internship proved successful and within weeks of starting, and prior to his college graduation, Adeli brought the young designer on a trip with her to Paris. When Adeli later moved her business to New York, Lim, however, decided to stay in California.

Phillip Lim's real success began then, in 2000, when he, along with partners Andy Crane and Stuart Gaddis, launched Development, a contemporary women's line. The Los Angeles-based company attracted a cult following for its simple, timeless pieces, but in 2004 the partners parted ways due to creative differences. The young designer was despondent, but as luck would have it, he remained unemployed for just twenty-four hours.

While designing for Development, Lim caught the eye of Wen Zhou, the CEO of a fabric company they worked with. The day after Lim lost his job at Development, Zhou called him, bought him a ticket to New York, and put up the money for them to start a company. Zhou and Lim, both thirty-one when the company was formed, named the label for their age, 3.1 Phillip Lim. Within six months, said Zhou, they "did 2.8 million in sales." And the profits didn't stop there. As it turned out, the designer had tapped into exactly what was missing in the fashion world at that time: classic designs with fashionable updates that sold at affordable prices.

For the Fall 2007 season, when the company hit $12 million in sales, Lim showed thirty-eight looks

for men and women. The collection, inspired by Edith Bouvier Beale and *Grey Gardens*, showed layers of preppy bow blouses, short shift dresses, and boxy boyfriend blazers. At a fraction of the cost of most designer pieces, 3.1 Phillip Lim was an instant hit, with the line selling at several major retailers, including Barneys New York. That same year, Lim opened his flagship store, a large retail space in New York's SoHo neighborhood. With an eyewear collection, a children's line, and several collaborations under his belt, *Vogue* editor-in-chief, Anna Wintour, wrote that Lim had "revolutionized what the fashion business knows as 'contemporary clothes'; i.e., clothes that are designer but don't break the bank."

By 2010, the unstoppable designer had created something of an empire. He had now launched a shoe line, lingerie, and swimwear, collaborated with the Gap and Uniqlo, and opened several more stores worldwide. For Spring 2010, Lim showed color, opening his runway show with a lipstick-red jacket and pants, "the new suit" as he called it. The end of the show revealed a series of cocktail dresses with various arrangements of pleats, panels, lace, and sequins, each perfect for a night out. The show, and Lim, proved that wearable clothes sell. For fall of the same year, Lim struck gold yet again with simplistic takes on seventies classics. A pair of sleek bell-bottoms was paired with a wool cape in camel, tan, and black. Purple sequins and gold pants suit also made appearances for Fall 2010, but there was no shortage of bestsellers, including several chic camel coats and more than a few festive asymmetrical dresses. Since the company began in 2004, Lim has mastered the art of creating chic, wearable clothing at a lower price point. With several awards and through-the-roof sales, Phillip Lim's influence in the industry has been confirmed.

1973 Born in Thailand
1991 Commences studies in home economics with specialization in fashion advertising at California State University, Long Beach
1998 Works as a design assistant at Katayone Adeli
1999 Designs for Paul Frank Industries
2000–04 Designs for Development
2005 Debuts 3.1 Phillip Lim
2007 Launches men's and childrens-wear; receives CFDA Swarovski Award for Womenswear; opens 3.1 Phillip Lim flagship store on New York's Mercer Street
2009 Introduces swimwear and a shoe line; presents first stand-alone menswear collection
2010 Opens a store in Singapore
2011 Nominated for CFDA Swarovski Award for Menswear

Phillip Lim, 2007

1949 Christian Dior founds
Christian Dior New York Inc.

1955 *East of Eden* with James Dean
is released in theaters

1962 Marilyn Monroe dies

1975 British punk band
The Sex Pistols forms

| 1930 | 1935 | 1940 | 1945 | 1950 | 1955 | 1960 | 1965 | 1970 | 1975 | 1980 |

Isabel Marant Spring/Summer 2005
Prêt-à-Porter show, Paris

1999 Tracey Emin's *My Bed* is
nominated for the Turner Prize

1982 Production of first
commercial CD player

1995 *Toy Story* is the first wholly
computer-generated film

2009 Michael Jackson dies

2016 Olympic Games in Rio de Janeiro

1985   1990   1995   2000   2005   2010   2015   2020   2025   2030   2035

ISABEL MARANT

Isabel Marant is the epitome of cool, French style. The designer, who was born in Paris in 1967 to a German model mother and a French father, consistently creates effortless pieces that are equal parts casual tomboy and sexy bohemian.

With the intent of creating clothing that set her apart, Marant learned to sew in her teens, later studying design at Studio Berçot. After school, Marant worked with Parisian designer Michel Klein, but left in 1989 to launch a collection of jewelry. Her full line of ready-to-wear came several years later, with influences from her vast childhood travels as well as an appreciation of tomboy style. Her first show, in 1994, was held in the courtyard of a squat and featured the designer's own friends as models. "I had set myself a simple goal," said Marant, "I wanted to create clothes that I myself wished to buy, clothes for girls, working women, who have taste and are willing to spend a little money on their looks without breaking the bank." She further proved her point in 2000 when she launched Étoile, a youthful collection that retained the spirit of her label, but sold at a slightly lower price point.

Isabel Marant's mix of tomboyish streetwear with ethnic, bohemian elements has proven to be the perfect formula, her pieces now coveted by women around the world. To help her achieve the sexy yet nonchalant look, Marant enlisted her childhood friend Emmanuelle Alt, then the fashion director at French *Vogue*, to style the collection. Until that point, in the late 2000s, Isabel Marant's desirable pieces had been quite exclusive, with boutiques only in Paris and limited stockists in America. But by the end of the decade, after she'd been in business for fifteen years, Marant's label took off with impressive speed.

Marant's Fall 2009 collection was the ideal blend of sophistication and relaxed chic, featuring menswear-inspired tweed jackets paired with slouchy trousers, miniskirts styled with casual T-shirts, and sexy printed dresses topped with fur coats. And then there were the shoes. Marant's suede over-the-knee boots and tough silver-studded booties were also stars of the show, instantly causing waiting lists at her shops. The following spring's fringed pairs added to the frenzy, selling out

from stores within hours. The Spring 2010 collection, with its cheerful pops of hot pink and multicolor pants with Lurex stripes, was inspired by imaginary bohemian travelers on a journey around the world, stopping to pick up pieces along the way.

The idea of world travel was still on her mind as Marant approached her Spring 2012 collection. Inspired by what a girl-on-the-go would pack in her fantasy suitcase for a summer away, Marant set to work creating the ultimate seasonal wardrobe for a fashionably earthy traveler. The sporty pieces, which included loose-fitting track pants, numbered football jersey-inspired T-shirts, and track jackets were mixed with bohemian elements such as colorful patchwork jeans, sexy tie-dyed dresses, and slouchy, textured knits.

With her new US flagship in New York and a store set to open in Los Angeles, Marant embraced her affinity for Americana with a western-inspired Fall 2012 collection. The feminine, ruffled silk miniskirts and the yoked cowboy blouses were paired with denim jackets embellished with studs and embroidery. Now famous for her jeans, Marant showed pairs in red, pink, and black, with everything from fringe and piping to floral embroidery.

With a loyal following of fashion editors and actresses, including Kate Bosworth, Kirsten Dunst, and Alexa Chung, Isabel Marant's enviable style has found its way to countless magazine spreads and street style blogs. Over the past few years, the label's advertisements have featured models such as Kate Moss, Arizona Muse, and Daria Werbowy, an impressive roster of faces for any brand. Marant's carefully constructed tousled look perfectly captures the feeling of effortless style, one that women around the world have strived to capture. Her pairing of tomboyish sexiness with relaxed, bohemian chic have made Isabel Marant the quintessentially cool Parisian designer.

1967 Born in Paris
1985–87 Studies design at Studio
Bercot fashion school
1987–89 Apprentices with Michel
Klein, Bridget Yorke, and
Marc Ascoli
1989 Launches jewelry collection
1990 Founds knitwear label Twen
with her mother
1994 Establishes her own label
1997 Wins Award de la Mode
1998 Launches I*M line in Japan;
opens her first store
1999 Introduces diffusion line, Étoile
2004 Childrenswear is introduced
2006 Collaborates with Anthropologie
2010 Opens store in New York
2012 Set to open store in L.A.

above
Isabel Marant, 2007

following double page
Isabel Marant Fall/Winter 2012/13
Prêt-à-Porter collection, Paris

1949 Elsa Schiaparelli opens a branch of
her fashion house in New York

1953 Hubert de Givenchy meets
Audrey Hepburn

1962 The Rolling Stones form

1967 The musical *Hair* premieres
off-Broadway in New York

1973 Pablo Picasso dies

1930　　1935　　1940　　1945　　1950　　1955　　1960　　1965　　1970　　1975　　1980

Marchesa Fall/Winter 2012/13 show,
New York Fashion Week

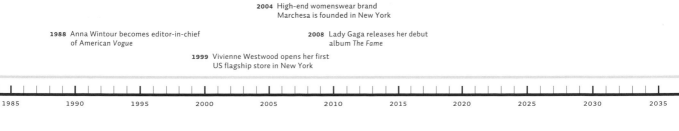

2004 High-end womenswear brand
Marchesa is founded in New York

1988 Anna Wintour becomes editor-in-chief
of American *Vogue*

2008 Lady Gaga releases her debut
album *The Fame*

1999 Vivienne Westwood opens her first
US flagship store in New York

1985   1990   1995   2000   2005   2010   2015   2020   2025   2030   2035

MARCHESA

Named for the scandalous twentieth-century socialite Luisa Casati, Georgina Chapman and Keren Craig's Marchesa line of high-end dresses has been dazzling since they first launched in 2004. The glamorous, highly intricate confections have developed a cult following and dominated the red carpet for almost a decade.

The designers of Marchesa met while both were students at the Chelsea College of Art and Design in London. Craig was born in 1976 in Lucerne, Switzerland, and graduated in 2000 from the Brighton Art College with a major in fashion textiles, focusing on print and embroidery. Her partner, Georgina Chapman, was born in London the same year, her father a millionaire and owner of an organic coffee company. Chapman began modeling in her twenties, appearing in various television shows and movies after graduating from Wimbledon School of Art in 2001.

In 2004, Chapman and Craig started Marchesa, and with Luisa Casati as their muse, they brought to life the eccentric aristocrat's vision of living life as a work of art. Soon after their couture-level line began, it became a favorite among celebrities, with elaborate dresses perfect for the red carpet. The label is centered on intricate cocktail attire, their detailed craftsmanship and touches of whimsy making Marchesa a favorite with the fashion press as well. It helps, no question, that Chapman and Craig, former model themselves, are often photographed in their designs.

In 2004, the pair set to work in Chapman's London flat, creating the first collection of custom-made pieces. That fall, Renée Zellweger wore a red-and-gold, sari-inspired Marchesa dress to the London premiere of *Bridget Jones: The Edge of Reason*, getting the line, then less than six months old, some major attention. By 2007, Marchesa had been worn by Cate Blanchett, Jennifer Lopez, and Sienna Miller, who wore a white feathery dress on the cover of *Vogue*. The designers staged their first runway show in September of that year, showing a romantic spring collection of twenty-six evening looks. The dresses, which came in white, black, pale lime green, light pink, and hot pink, were abloom with floral details. The opening look was a pale pink minidress featuring a row of flowers along the bust.

At the end of 2007, Chapman married her boyfriend of three years, film producer Harvey Weinstein, wearing an ivory tulle Marchesa dress that she designed for the occasion. The designers had also started a diffusion collection called Notte by Marchesa, which consisted of cocktail and evening dresses at a lower price point. Their glamorous creations for Marchesa continued season after season, with countless celebrities wearing the label for Hollywood events. For Spring 2010, the collection referenced Madame Butterfly. There were kimono-style satin gowns and sculptural ruffles made from horsehair, as well as a stunning "Grecian draped column partly masked with carefully beaded black lace."

For the Spring 2012 and Fall 2012 collections, Marchesa reverted back to a traditional runway show format (their past several seasons had been presentations with models standing on podiums). Spring showed several flapperesque fringe dresses, while fall was inspired by William-Adolphe Bouguereau's *A Soul Brought to Heaven*, a nineteenth-century French painting depicting two angels carrying a woman into the clouds. The clothes reflected the work in their intricate embroideries, feather petticoats, and ruffled tulle skirts.

Vogue may have put it best when they said, "If Fashion Week is like high school, Marchesa is the prom queen. She doesn't even have to compete like everyone else—she just prettily reigns." Meaning, despite not following in fashion trends, the label has managed to achieve a cult following, especially on the red carpet. After seeing their dresses in 2006, the late fashion icon Isabella Blow said to Chapman and Craig, "Girls, no one is doing this; you must do more." And, luckily, they listened, much to the delight of starlets and fashion critics alike.

1976 Georgina Chapman born in London on April 14; Keren Craig born in Lucerne on February 27
1995 Chapman and Craig meet at Chelsea College of Art & Design
2000 Keren Craig graduates from Brighton Art College
2001 Georgina Chapman graduates from Wimbledon School of Art
2004 Georgina Chapman and Keren Craig found Marchesa; Renée Zellweger wears Marchesa to the premiere of *Bridget Jones: The Edge of Reason*
2006 Launch diffusion line, Notte by Marchesa; Marchesa named one of the CFDA/Vogue Fashion Fund's top ten finalists
2007 First runway show; Marchesa worn by Sienna Miller on the cover of Vogue
2009 Launches a full bridal collection
2010 Marchesa launches a collection of evening bags

Georgina Chapman of Marchesa, 2011

left
Marchesa presentation,
New York Bridal Week, 2011

right
Marchesa Spring/Summer
2011 show, New York Fashion
Week

1940 The first McDonald's restaurant opens

1954 Pierre Cardin opens his first boutique in Paris

1972 Diane von Furstenberg founds her eponymous fashion label

1964 British fashion clothing retailer Topshop is founded

| 1930 | 1935 | 1940 | 1945 | 1950 | 1955 | 1960 | 1965 | 1970 | 1975 | 1980 |

Erdem Fall/Winter 2008/09 collection, London Fashion Week

1999 Prada takes over the fashion houses
of Jil Sander and Helmut Lang

1998 Google is founded

1989 First electronic dance music festival
Love Parade in Berlin

2011 Royal Wedding of Prince William of
Wales and Catherine Middleton

2007 The final book of the *Harry Potter*
series is released

| 1985 | 1990 | 1995 | 2000 | 2005 | 2010 | 2015 | 2020 | 2025 | 2030 | 2035 |

ERDEM MORALIOGLU

Erdem Moralioglu, the half Turkish, half English designer, has become known for his delicate dresses and beautiful florals, creating an elegant, romantic aesthetic that is feminine at its core.

The designer was born in Canada in 1977 and raised on Lake Saint-Louis with his twin sister Sara. He moved to London in 2000 to study at the Royal College of Art and after graduating moved to New York to work with Diane von Furstenberg. One year later, however, he moved back to London's East End to start his own line, Erdem (the designer goes by just his first name in life, as well). The imaginative debut collection received critical acclaim and won Erdem the Fashion Fringe award, along with a substantial prize.

For his third collection following the award, Erdem showed a series of beautiful and refined pieces. The Spring 2007 collection was filled with dresses embellished by embroidery and intricate laces, as well as offbeat prints of flowers and birds. To temper the preciousness, Erdem mixed in cleaner sportswear elements, including a tan belted raincoat (made in collaboration with Mackintosh, the traditional British coat company) and a pair of classic pleated trousers. He showed the collection in the fall of 2006, the same year that supermodel Claudia Schiffer wore one of his dresses to the British Academy of Film and Television awards and Julie Gilhart, then Barneys fashion director, wore another to the Met Ball. It was no coincidence that Gilhart, a supporter of emerging talent in the industry, had recently placed a large order with Erdem, making Barneys the label's largest international stockist.

Erdem is not one to be influenced by fleeting trends. Instead, the designer has said, "I never think about what's sexy. I focus on the silhouettes and the proportions and hope that takes care of everything." For his Spring 2009 collection, Erdem pushed the limits of prettiness, showing pastel-hued dresses of French lace and watercolor-inspired prints of flowers. "I just wanted something soft and hyper-romantic, easy but a bit surreal at the same time," said Erdem of the collection, which was inspired by seventies theater productions of

Shakespeare. The silhouettes drew reference from Edwardian dresses, with their high necks and layers of ruffles. Erdem's designs were exquisite, with critics comparing his workmanship to haute couture.

For the following spring, he continued to show florals, but the intense color and vivid prints of this collection were perfectly sharp, with nothing blurred or soft. Erdem's opening look, which drew reference from Japanese art and culture, was a garden of embroidered pansies in intense shades of yellow and purple. The signature feminine elements were all still firmly in place, to which the designer said, "I never really do theme. I always think it should just be like reading the next chapter of the same book."

Art has also been a major influence for Erdem. For his Fall 2011 collection, the designer found his inspiration in an unhinged artist's wife, who had ripped apart paintings and made them into clothing. The collection was darker than usual, in both palette and spirit, the fifties shapes crafted from unusual fabrics with odd areas of embellishment. Like the Abstract Expressionists themselves, whose work was fully referenced in Erdem's collection, the clothes were dark, but not without incredible beauty. The artistic narrative continued for the following fall, with the collection shown in London's new White Cube gallery. The inspiration, the designer explained, was still the strong, dark woman of the previous year, but her rage had subsided. This muse was an art collector, not its destroyer. For Fall 2012, Erdem continued his exploration of mixing materials, this time combining provocative rubber latex with lace and tweed.

"I see each collection as a new chapter in the same book of her life," Erdem has said of his label's muse. "It's a narrative, but she's still the same core girl: colorful, sweet, elegant and hopefully effortless." And Erdem's narrative is one that the fashion industry and the consumer alike keep going back to, eager to see what inventive confections the next season will bring.

1977 Born in Montreal on August 31
1995 Enrolls in bachelor's program in fashion at Ryerson University, Toronto
2000 Moves to London; interns with Vivienne Westwood
2001–03 Master's degree at Royal College of Art
2004 Moves to New York; works with Diane Von Furstenberg
2005 Founds Erdem in East London; runway debut at Fashion Fringe
2006 Begins collaboration with Mackintosh
2007 Receives Swarovski British Fashion Council Fashion Enterprise Award
2009 Collaborates with Globe-Trotter, Cutler and Gross, and Smythson
2010 Wins British Fashion Council/Vogue Designer Fashion Fund Award

Erdem, 2009

left
Erdem Spring/Summer 2012
show, London Fashion Week

right
Erdem Spring/Summer 2009
show, London Fashion Week

1943 Shoe designer Manolo Blahnik
is born

1955 James Dean dies

1962 Andy Warhol paints
Campbell's Soup Cans

1977 Jimmy Carter
sworn in as 39t
US president

1951 J. D. Salinger's *The Catcher
in the Rye* is published

1930　　1935　　1940　　1945　　1950　　1955　　1960　　1965　　1970　　1975　　1980

Richard Nicoll Spring/Summer 2011
collection

1989 Animated TV sitcom
The Simpsons debuts

1986 Marc Jacobs presents his
first collection

2007 First Berlin Fashion Week

1999 Larry and Andy Wachowski's
The Matrix is released in theaters

1985 1990 1995 2000 2005 2010 2015 2020 2025 2030 2035

RICHARD NICOLL

Coined the "King of the Blouse" by New York Times fashion writer Suzy Menkes in 2006, Richard Nicoll has become one of London's most notable designers. The designer, who lives in London and grew up in Australia, references both places in menswear-inspired collections.

Specifically, it was his pin-tucked blouses paired with tailored pants and crisp shorts that inspired Menkes to call the young designer "a hot new talent." Nicoll was born in 1975 in London. His parents, both originally from New Zealand, moved to Australia when their son was still quite young, enrolling him at Scotch College, a boarding school for boys in Perth. While in school, Nicoll shopped at thrift stores, trying to differentiate his daily uniform, but the standard-issue pieces made an impact, serving as inspiration for the designer's later collections.

In 1996 Nicoll moved back to London to study at Central Saint Martins, where his aesthetic developed. "A bit London, a bit Australian, and a bit fantasy," the designer said of his style. The look, based on menswear-inspired pieces and Victoriana, is topped off with an "optimistic and playful" spirit that Nicoll credits to his Australian roots. In 2002, Nicoll graduated with a Master's degree in womenswear, but the real success came after, when his entire graduate collection was bought by Dolce & Gabbana. Then, following shows at Fashion East during London Fashion Week and freelance work for Marc Jacobs at Louis Vuitton, the designer established his own signature label in 2005.

Nicoll's first solo show, for Fall 2006, was inspired by Victorian housemaids, but the collection was far from traditional, with original plays on the historical garb. The unexpected combinations of shirts tied at the neck with black bows paired with biker jackets and tight, layered bodices were met with rave reviews, critics noting that the beautifully crafted separates would be very wearable on their own. The shirts stood out, with several variations shown in Nicoll's twenty-five look collection. Over the next two years, Nicoll designed costumes for Kylie Minogue's 2006 tour, designed guest collections for Topshop, and won the British Fashion Council Fashion Forward Award two years in a row. It was clear that Nicoll's star was rapidly rising. Then in 2009 Nicoll was named the creative director

of Cerruti, a logical choice based on the history of the brand. In the 1970s, founder Nino Cerruti made using men's fabrics for womenswear a popular trend. Nicoll has described his line for Cerruti as "structured clothes with femininity" for an "active working woman." Sadly, Nicoll's time at Cerruti was brief, as the house decided to stop producing womenswear after the Fall 2011 collection.

His departure from Cerruti only allowed Nicoll to focus more deeply on his own label. For Spring 2012 and Fall 2012, the designer looked to film for his references, using Henri-Georges Clouzot's *L'Enfer* and Charlie Chaplin's *Modern Times*, respectively. For spring, he mixed the sixties mod look of Clouzot's unfinished film with elements of David Lynch, such as the prominent color of underwater flowers that he dubbed "Laura Palmer blue," for Lynch's *Twin Peaks* character. He described the look as "saccharine and psychedelic," the range of blues and the mod shapes accompanied by Nicoll's signature wit and a dash of futurism. He followed up the next season with a collection based on the production line, referencing Chaplin's silent film *Modern Times*, and Jacques Tati's *Play Time*. The silhouettes were simple and straight, but with a bold palette of orange, blue, and yellow. Of the season, which was based on the idea of clothes for work, Nicoll said, "It's my favorite collection ever." The suits, smocks, and pleated shift dresses were straight to the point, embodying the essence of utilitarian clothing.

Richard Nicoll's label has always been one to push boundaries while remaining true to its menswear-inspired roots. The designer put it best when he said his goal is to create "democratic, idiosyncratic clothes for life."

1975 Born in London
1996–2002 Studies sculpture, menswear, and womenswear at Central Saint Martins
2002 Dolce & Gabbana purchase his graduate presentation
2003 Debuts his collection at London Fashion Week
2005 Founds Richard Nicoll label; starts designing for Topshop
2007 Wins three ANDAM Awards and second British Fashion Council Fashion Forward Award; collaborates with Ksubi and Topman
2008 Wins Best Young Designer at British Elle Style Awards
2009 Becomes creative director at Cerruti
2010 Introduces diffusion line at Cerruti

Richard Nicoll

left
Richard Nicoll Fall/Winter 2012/13
collection

right
Richard Nicoll Fall/Winter 2012/13
collection

1945 French designer Pierre Balmain
opens a house of couture in Paris

1957 *On the Road* by Jack Kerouac
is published

1974 Performance *I Like America
and America Likes Me* by
Joseph Beuys in New York

1964 British fashion clothing retailer
Topshop is founded

1930   1935   1940   1945   1950   1955   1960   1965   1970   1975   1980

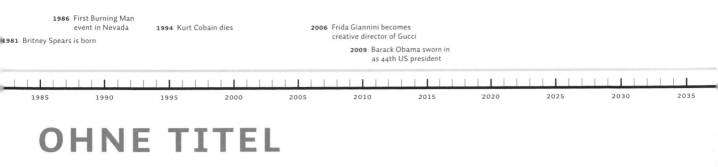

1986 First Burning Man event in Nevada		**1994** Kurt Cobain dies	**2006** Frida Giannini becomes creative director of Gucci		
1981 Britney Spears is born			**2009** Barack Obama sworn in as 44th US president		

1985   1990   1995   2000   2005   2010   2015   2020   2025   2030   2035

OHNE TITEL

Ohne Titel, German for "untitled," may be the perfect name for Alexa Adams and Flora Gills' low-profile label. The best friends who founded their line in 2006 have remained relatively out of the spotlight, choosing instead to focus on design.

The pair both graduated from Parsons School of Design in 2002, creating pieces together during their senior year, a small collection they've dubbed as their "unofficial first." After graduation, they went on to work with other designers—Adams worked for Helmut Lang, and then they both worked under Karl Lagerfeld. Their runway debut was in September 2007 at New York Fashion Week, a collection inspired by safari pieces and the work of artist Jean Dubuffet, whose textured paintings were often enhanced with materials such as tar and straw. The star of the show was their suiting, the draped asymmetric jackets shown in white, tan, and a soft lipstick red; but added to their printed knits and sculptural pieces were raffia and rubber accessories that they designed themselves.

Their interest in suits carried into the next season as the designers were contemplating "how suits relate to women," and thinking about the articles of clothing that feel most empowering. The inspiration came, in large part, from the Democratic primaries of 2008 that positioned Hillary Clinton as a possible candidate for the upcoming presidential race. Ohne Titel's beautifully draped suits came, this season, in shades of red, rich tans, and deep cobalt blues. Some critics feared that the collection was too similar to their last, but Adams explained that, as designers, they're "mainly trying to eliminate categories … the idea of seasons and day vs. night. [People] want an adaptable wardrobe, especially now."

Adams and Gill really hit their stride for Spring 2011, when they drew inspiration from Japanese package design and the woodcuts of artist Utagawa Kuniyoshi. The collection came in black, white, and navy with some sparse pops of royal blue and brighter accents on the accessories. The necklaces were part of a collaboration with artist Tauba Auerbach, a friend of the duo who had previously modeled for their campaigns. There was a futuristic sleekness to the collection, as well as a distinct sportiness that came from the neoprene bodysuits and the graphic colorblocked patterns. The bold striping came largely from varying textures, including rubber-coated yarn and glazed leather.

For Fall 2011, they drew reference from astronauts, taking the best elements of space suits and incorporating them into textured dresses and strong hooded coats. "We were intrigued by the way they morph what we think of as normal proportions on the body," said Adams of their fascination with space suits. They again experimented with mixed materials, using varieties of fur, leather, and heavy knits on their extraordinarily luxe coats. In shades of black and gray with buckles and curly lamb fur at the collar, the coats exuded confidence and a hefty does of style.

They followed up with a more colorful and playful collection for Spring 2012, which included draped colorblocked dresses that, while strong and graphic, had more feminine flounce than previous seasons. They retained their sporty influence, as well, with athletic drawstring pants, leather jackets, and cropped sweaters. The departure was brief, however, and the designers returned to a tougher look for Fall 2012. Their mostly black and white fall collection of just twenty-two looks was inspired by artist Sheila Hicks, who had incorporated newspaper into her work. The clothes, which referenced ideas of armor in their architectural-like forms, still integrated elements of Ohne Titel's now renowned luxury. There were two-tone pleated skirts, heavy fur coats, and several of the label's signature knits.

Though Alexa Adams and Flora Gill are relatively quiet when it comes to press and branding, their clothes have spoken for them, and the message they've delivered is one of timeless female strength and mixed-media luxury.

1999   Alexa Adams and Flora Gill meet at Parsons School of Design
2002   Graduate from Parsons
2005   The pair both work for Karl Lagerfeld
2006   Found their label, Ohne Titel
2007   Debut collection of womenswear at New York Fashion Week in September
2008   Work with Cesare Paciotti to produce shoe collection
2009   Receive the Ecco Domani Fashion Foundation Award

opposite page
Ohne Titel Fall/Winter 2012/13
collection 2012

above
Flora Gill and Alexa Adams of
Ohne Titel

Ohne Titel Fall/Winter 2012/13 collection

1944 French fashion designer
Paul Poiret dies

1955 *East of Eden* with James Dean
is released in theaters

1965 Emanuel Ungaro opens a
haute-couture salon in Paris

1971 Photographer Larry Clark
publishes his book *Tulsa*

1930 1935 1940 1945 1950 1955 1960 1965 1970 1975 1980

Thakoon Spring 2012 Prêt-à-Porter collection,
New York Fashion Week

1999 Prada takes over the fashion houses
of Jil Sander and Helmut Lang

1988 Anna Wintour becomes editor-in-chief
of American *Vogue*

2004 Founding of Facebook

1981 Beyoncé Knowles is born

2007 The Apple iPhone goes on sale

| 1985 | 1990 | 1995 | 2000 | 2005 | 2010 | 2015 | 2020 | 2025 | 2030 | 2035 |

THAKOON PANICHGUL

Though he had been praised by the fashion industry for years, Thakoon Panichgul's label, Thakoon, became known across America in 2008, when Michelle Obama wore one of his dresses—a thoroughly modern design with vibrant bursts of red and purple—in front of millions.

The dress was perfect for the fashion-forward Obama to wear as her husband accepted the Democratic nomination for the presidency. Subsequently, in her very public role as first lady, Obama has worn several pieces by the Thai-born designer, keeping his name consistently in the public's eye. Michelle Obama aside, Thakoon has become known for its sophisticated separates and flattering dresses.

Panichgul was born in Nakhon Phanom Province, Thailand in 1974, and moved with his family to the United States when he was eleven years old. The family settled in Omaha, Nebraska, and after graduating from Boston University with a business degree in 1997, Panichgul moved to New York. He began as a fashion writer, which cultivated a love of design and four years later he enrolled at Parsons School of Design. He graduated in 2003 and by the fall of the following year he produced and showed his first collection. The first collection, for Spring 2005, consisted of just ten pieces, but the modern looks received excellent reviews. Of the collection, which included linen shorts and an embroidered taffeta coat, Panichgul said "I think that fashion is entering into a new kind of formality—one that is spirited and space age, rather than stuffy and boring."

For Spring 2006, Panichgul staged his first full runway show, aiming for something "modern and pretty in a twinkling kind of way." The show opened with a lovely white organza dress, followed by a series of weightless, gauzy looks and details such as delicately tied knots on dresses and shorts. His show continued with shimmering metallic silks in gold and silver, as well as a blue diamond print and smaller details such as crystal buttons. The jewel conceit proved successful—fashion editors and buyers alike praised the ethereal Thakoon show.

By 2007, Thakoon had been singled out by Anna Wintour and *Vogue* as one of the important American labels and the designer was commissioned to produce a line for the Gap. His looks were also making a big splash on the red carpet, with celebrities like Sarah Jessica Parker, Drew Barrymore, and Demi Moore wearing Thakoon to events and premieres. Then, in 2009, Panichgul designed a limited edition collection for Target, which sold out almost immediately. Between the press received from Michelle Obama and a cameo appearance in *The September Issue*, by the end of the decade Thakoon was one of New York's best-known labels.

Panichgul is constantly exploring different cultures and areas of the world. For Spring 2010, his signature print dresses were shown alongside kimono-inspired pieces. The following year, for Fall 2011, Panichgul's collection was based on the similarities in the clothes of Versailles and the items worm by Masai warriors in Kenya. The concept manifested itself in the shape of ball skirts done in yellow batik and bustled vests in red-and-blue buffalo plaid. This fresh collection, with its far-flung references and mismatched prints was, as Panichgul put it, "fanciful, but pavement." In other words, the collection, while undoubtedly high-concept, felt sporty and thoroughly modern. Panichgul kept the momentum alive the following season with yet another mash-up, this time inspired by a mix of classic Western apparel and traditional Indian motifs. The vibrant collection, with a range of colors from gold and orange to turquoise, included Western shirts and metallic-trimmed saris. Embroidered necklines on colorful paisley dresses combined the best of both worlds.

Thakoon Panichgul's fresh approach to design concepts and his innate knowledge of what women want to wear has turned the label into an important force in fashion. Each season both the fashion industry and consumers alike anxiously await the latest Thakoon collection, eager to discover what the talented designer has in store.

1974 Born in Chiang Rai Province, Thailand

1997 Graduates with a business degree from Boston University

2001 Takes classes at Parsons School of Design

2004 Debuts Thakoon line at New York Fashion Week

2006 Receives the Vogue/CFDA Fashion Fund Award

2007 Collaborates on a collection of white shirts for the Gap

2008 Inducted into the Council of Fashion Designers of America (CFDA); Michelle Obama wears Thakoon to the final night of the Democratic National Convention

2007–09 Designs for Hogan

2009 His collection for Target released in store; he appears in *The September Issue*; establishes diffusion line, Thakoon Addition; becomes creative director at Tasaki

Thakoon Panichgul, 2011

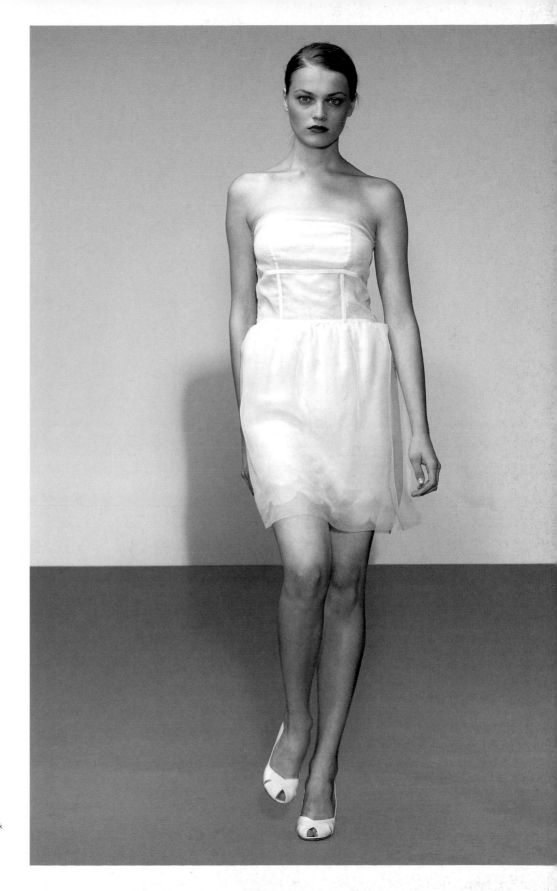

left
Thakoon Fall/Winter 2012/13
collection, New York Fashion Week

right
Thakoon Spring 2006 collection,
Olympus Fashion Week, New York

1930   1935   1940   1945   1950   1955   1960   1965   1970   1975   1980

Dita Von Teese, Zac Posen Fall 2011 show,
Mercedes-Benz Fashion Week, New York

1982 Release of Madonna's debut single "Everybody"

1993 Bill Clinton sworn in as 42nd US president

2001 Wikipedia is launched

2011 Amy Winehouse dies

1997 Animated TV sitcom *South Park* debuts

1985   1990   1995   2000   2005   2010   2015   2020   2025   2030   2035

ZAC POSEN

While his bio reads a bit like a who's who of the downtown New York scene, Zac Posen, born in 1980, has proved his design skills. Now known, and loved, for feminine party dresses, Posen's glamorous aesthetic is perhaps most at home on the red carpet.

Born and raised in SoHo by his artist father, Stephen Posen, and lawyer mother, Susan Posen, Zac attended Saint Ann's, a private school in Brooklyn. His classmates there included actress Paz de la Huerta and Stella Schnabel, the daughter of painter Julian Schnabel. He befriended both and by the end of high school, the well-photographed young It-girls were wearing his designs out on the town. His social connections paid off in 2000, when a dress originally made for Naomi Campbell was spotted on sixteen-year-old Paz de la Huerta and, in turn, borrowed by actress Jade Malle, who wore the bias-cut, pink silk confection to Kate Hudson's wedding. All of the press and the buzz surrounding this swooping, brushed silk dress occurred when Posen was just twenty years old, still a fashion design student at Central Saint Martins College of Art and Design.

Posen began making clothes for his dolls at age four and costumes for his school plays as a teenager. His first commission was at fifteen, when Stella Schnabel, a few years his junior, asked Posen to make her a dress for an event that when photographed would look as if she was naked.

Posen's roots certainly have their share of glamour, but the young designer also worked hard to learn his craft. In 1996, Posen landed a coveted internship at the Costume Collection at the Metropolitan Museum of Art where he worked closely for long-time curator Richard Martin while taking courses at the Parsons School of Design. Shortly after, as an intern at Nicole Miller's studio, one of Posen's designs was selected to go into production. One year later, and just out of high school, Posen became a design assistant at Tocca, an influential label at the time. After he was accepted to the prestigious Central Saint Martins, Posen moved from New York to London to continue his design studies. While in London, a leather gown he created was displayed in the *Curvaceous* exhibition at the Victoria and Albert Museum.

In 2001, Posen moved back to New York. The next winter, he showed his first runway during New York Fashion Week. The independently produced show included a mix of bigger name models—Karen Elson, Liberty Ross, Sophie Dahl—alongside Posen's own friends Paz de la Huerta and Jemima Kirke. The collection, for Fall 2002, had been inspired by 1930s cocktail fashion and was met with good reviews. Posen's colorful, monochrome palette was paired with formal materials, like satins and crepes, and the evening dresses featured several deep-V necklines.

Posen's strong yet womanly aesthetic has been a favorite of young celebrities for the past decade. Natalie Portman, who Posen has publically called his muse, wore one of his dresses to the 2002 premiere of *Star Wars: Episode II—Attack of the Clones*.

Posen's success continued, but the economic downturn hit his business hard, prompting the designer to expand into producing more affordable collections. He began producing Z Spoke for Saks Fifth Avenue and in 2010 he designed a capsule collection in collaboration with mass-market retailer Target. The collection focused on dresses and prints with several reinterpretations of key pieces from Posen's brand. His flirty party dresses and feminine tuxedo suits were now all available, thanks to Target, for under $200 a piece.

With Z Spoke showing in New York, Posen decided to move his signature line to Paris for Spring 2011, taking up residence in a venue where Yves Saint Laurent used to show. The evening pieces were met with mixed reviews and his stay in Paris was short-lived; for Spring 2012 Posen returned to his native New York. The Spring 2012 collection focused on the waist—nipped jackets were paired with chic pencil skirts. Posen had returned to his roots, sending several glamorous party dresses down the runway. The flared skirts and off-the-shoulder tops were red-carpet ready, perfect for the young starlets that Posen has proved so good at dressing.

Zac Posen, 2011

1980 Born in New York City on October 24
1994 Takes pre-college courses at Parsons School of Design
1996–98 Interns with Richard Martin at the Metropolitan Museum of Art's Costume Institute
1998 Interns for Nicole Miller
1999 Moves to London to attend Central Saint Martins
2001 Drops out of school and returns to New York; presents first collection; Henri Bendel begins selling his line
2002 Wins Ecco Domani Fashion Foundation Award; stages his first independent runway show; Bloomingdale's showcases his work in windows
2004 Wins CFDA Swarovski Perry Ellis Award
2005 Collaborates with Wolford and Jaguar; introduces Zac Posen for Seven for All Mankind at Neiman Marcus
2010 Shows his signature collection in Paris and begins producing Z Spoke
2012 Brings his runway show back to New York Fashion Week

1945 Marilyn Monroe discovered
as a photo model

1954 Pierre Cardin opens his
first boutique in Paris

1972 Diane von Furstenberg
founds her fashion label
Diane von Furstenberg

1969 Woodstock Festival

| 1930 | 1935 | 1940 | 1945 | 1950 | 1955 | 1960 | 1965 | 1970 | 1975 | 1980 |

Preen by Thornton Bregazzi, London Fashion Week, 2012

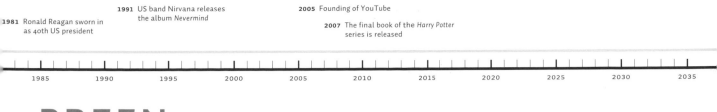

1983 Karl Lagerfeld becomes the
artistic director of Chanel

1991 US band Nirvana releases
the album *Nevermind*

2005 Founding of YouTube

1981 Ronald Reagan sworn in
as 40th US president

2007 The final book of the *Harry Potter*
series is released

1985   1990   1995   2000   2005   2010   2015   2020   2025   2030   2035

PREEN

Justin Thornton and Thea Bregazzi are partners in all aspects of life. The pair met at age eighteen on the Isle of Man, an island in the Irish Sea, where they both grew up, and now, more than a decade after founding their line, Preen by Thornton and Bregazzi, the design duo and couple are still going strong.

After college, Thornton began designing the 2nd Life collection for designer Helen Storey, while Bregazzi worked as a stylist, occasionally designing pieces upon special commission. Then, in 1996, the pair was asked to consult for Helen Storey on her upcoming collection, leading to their first design collaboration. The result was pure success, inspiring Thornton and Bregazzi to launch their own line together.

They began in a slightly roundabout manner, setting up shop in Notting Hill, London in 1997 and selling exclusive, one-off pieces. Their custom, one-of-a-kind creations were an instant hit, flying off the racks at the pair's tiny Portobello Road boutique. With sales momentum on their side, Thornton and Bregazzi staged their first fashion show, for Spring/Summer 2001, at London Fashion Week. This first Preen show, a distinctly British mix of tongue-in-cheek looks, received rave reviews. The clothes mixed punk elements, including leather and lace, with their usual blend of masculine and feminine elements. Over the course of the next seven years, Preen became a favorite on the London fashion scene, revisiting themes of Victoriana, recycling, and deconstruction in their collections.

For Spring 2008, the Preen designers left their hometown to show at New York Fashion Week. Their stateside debut received ample buzz and the clothes did not disappoint. The season before, the pair had debuted an eighties-inspired display of neons and zippers, parachute pants and bodysuits, but they approached spring, and New York, with a softer collection. The colors were soft and feminine—lavender, white, pale yellow, and sand—with brighter moments of orange and blue and a few choice blacks. The fluid, draping silks were sporty and relaxed, balanced perfectly by the more body-conscious dresses.

That same year, the British design duo launched Preen Line, a contemporary diffusion line that allowed them to "show the two different sides of the label." The beautifully draped dresses and bandage-style pieces are infused with a distinct rock-and-roll element. Preen Line, they have said, gave the Preen customer "something for every day … for work or relaxed evenings."

With two lines stocked in thirty-five different countries worldwide, the designers now create six collections per year. For their Spring 2012 collection, Thornton and Bregazzi were inspired by Virginia Woolf, but they wanted to modernize their muse and they did so by scanning a classic romantic floral through a computer. The result was a digital, pixilated print imposed on several sophisticated, streamlined silhouettes. A series of feminine pastels opened the show with checkerboards of colors including bubblegum pink, sky blue, and lemon yellow. The show was not without Preen's usual subversion, despite the saccharine palette and several ruffled details. Unlike Preen's Fall 2011 season, which featured a geometric floral motif on tailored, menswear-inspired pieces, spring was a true departure into a more overtly feminine arena.

Despite a consistent play with deconstruction and the fusion of masculine and feminine elements, Preen's pieces are undeniably sophisticated and wearable. Their looks have not only graced the runways in two continents, but have been worn by trendsetters such as Kate Moss, Gwyneth Paltrow, and Beyoncé. With copious industry recognition, a loyal following of wearers, and a distinct individual style, Justin Thornton and Thea Bregazzi have built Preen into a truly cool and desirable contemporary label.

1968 Thea Bregazzi born on Isle of Man
1969 Justin Thornton born on the opposite end of the thirty-two-mile-long island
1987 Thornton and Bregazzi meet in school
1996 They first design together when asked to consult by Helen Storey; the same year, they launch Preen
1997 Open shop in Portobello Road
1998 Second store opens in Notting Hill, London; they start selling wholesale
1999 Selling in Tokyo
2001 Preen debuts at London Fashion Week
2007 Decamp from London to New York Fashion Week; begin collaborating with Topshop
2008 The pair launch the lower-priced Preen Line in February

Thea Bregazzi and Justin Thornton
of Preen, 2012

1947 Swedish retail-clothing company
Hennes & Mauritz is founded

1958 Truman Capote publishes his
novel *Breakfast at Tiffany's*

1969 Stonewall Uprising on
Christopher Street in New York

1976 Helmut Newton
publishes his first
photography book,
White Women

| 1930 | 1935 | 1940 | 1945 | 1950 | 1955 | 1960 | 1965 | 1970 | 1975 | 1980 |

Accessories jewelry detail on the runway
at the Proenza Schouler Spring/Summer 2011
show, New York Fashion Week

1985 Live Aid charity concert for famine relief in Africa

1988 Anna Wintour becomes editor-in-chief of American Vogue

1995 Launch of the Japanese electronic toy Tamagotchi

2003 Jean Paul Gaultier becomes creative director of Hermès

2010 World Expo in Shanghai

1985   1990   1995   2000   2005   2010   2015   2020   2025   2030   2035

PROENZA SCHOULER

The story of Proenza Schouler is the stuff of fashion legend. It started when two Parsons juniors, Jack McCollough and Lazaro Hernandez, asked to do their final thesis project together. Within weeks of presenting, Barneys' fashion director ordered the entire collection for a fall delivery just four months away.

The students, realizing that this was a once-in-a-lifetime opportunity, scrambled to produce the pieces and struggled to create a name for their new label. They settled on Proenza Schouler, a combination of their mothers' maiden names. With the Barneys order in the works and a credit in *Vogue* shot by Helmut Newton, the young designers, then twenty-three years old, never returned to school and never received their Parsons degrees.

The designers, who met at a bar in 1999 while both at Parsons, came to New York via two very different stories. McCollough, born in 1978, was raised in New Jersey, one of five children in a strict, conservative family. Kicked out of high school, the rowdy teen wound up in a boarding school, following a few months on the road touring with the Grateful Dead. It was there that he studied art and painting, falling in love with Gauguin and Van Gogh. Following boarding school, he studied at the San Francisco Art Institute and transferred to Parsons the following year. While in school, McCollough interned at Marc Jacobs, where he learned about the world of design.

Lazaro Hernandez, an only child, was born the same year, but grew up in Miami. His Cuban parents were more relaxed and each day after school he would go with his mother to her beauty salons, where he was introduced to fashion by flipping through magazines. Following the wishes of his parents, he began studying to be a doctor, but in his second year of pre-med in Florida he secretly applied to Parsons. He was accepted and moved to New York, where he studied design and later interned at Michael Kors (an internship he acquired after slipping a note to Anna Wintour on a plane).

The pair began dating during their junior year at Parsons, around the time that they began collaborating closely on their designs. Their partnership is just that; there is no hierarchy or division of labor, only an equal relationship that has resulted in some of the most exciting designs to come out of New York in the past decade. For their first runway show at New York Fashion Week for Fall 2003, the young designers showed a chic and polished collection. Muted black and brown coats mixed with sexy metallic bustiers creating a collection that felt sophisticated, yet young and fresh. "I think we're really attracted to contrasts," McCollough said in an interview with Ingrid Sischy, "You have shine and mattedness, masculine and feminine, big and small." That style, a mix of strong layers and slinky feminine pieces, became the Proenza Schouler signature and in 2004 they won the CFDA/Vogue Fashion Fund Award along with $200,000 to build their company.

Over the course of the decade the designers expanded their brand to include resort and pre-fall collections, along with a large shoe and bag business. As business grew, so too did the designers' vision. Their look was still effortlessly chic—a mix of sharp tailoring and fresh sportswear that had gained them a strong following among the New York It-girls.

For Spring 2010, they took inspiration from surfing, mixing their signature bra-cup bustier tops with neon tie-dye prints. Before the collection, as they do each season, the designers took a trip. This time they landed in Bora Bora, far from the pressures of the fashion industry, and returned inspired by the colors of fish they had seen while snorkeling. To prepare for their Fall 2010 collection, the duo took a road trip from New Mexico to Wyoming. Back in New York, they digitized and pixilated prints from Native American blankets they bought along the way, imposing the colorful patterns on cocktail dresses and slouchy pants. As with their surf collection the season before, the result was pure cool sophistication with an exploration of craft and a mastery of technique. Season after season, the designers of Proenza Schouler continue to draw inspiration from the world around them and, perhaps more importantly, from each other.

1978 Jack McCollough born in Tokyo; Lazaro Hernandez born in Miami
1999 Jack McCollough and Lazaro Hernandez meet at Parsons School of Design in New York
2000 Junior year, McCollough interns with Marc Jacobs; Lazaro asks Anna Wintour for help and receives an internship with Michael Kors
2002 The pair graduate from Parsons having been named designer of the year; their entire graduate collection is bought by Julie Gilhart of Barneys New York
2003 Proenza Schouler debuts at New York Fashion Week
2004 Wins the CFDA/Vogue Fashion Fund Award
2007 Proenza Schouler wins the CFDA Womenswear Designer of the Year Award; creates a capsule collection for Target
2008 Proenza Schouler introduces a shoe collection
2009 Wins CFDA Accessory Designer of the Year

Jack McCollough and Lazaro Hernandez of Proenza Schouler

left
Proenza Schouler Spring 2010
show, New York

right
Proenza Schouler Fall 2012
show, Mercedes-Benz Fashion
Week, New York

1951 J. D. Salinger's *The Catcher in the Rye* is published

1943 Premiere of *Casablanca*, directed by Michael Curtiz

1962 Andy Warhol paints *Campbell's Soup Cans*

1977 New York nightclub Studio 54 opens

1930 1935 1940 1945 1950 1955 1960 1965 1970 1975 1980

Gareth Pugh show at London Fashion Week, 2008

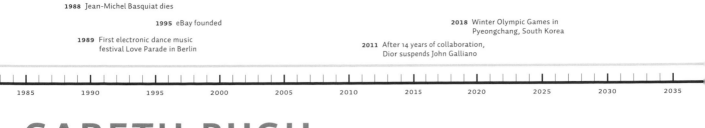

1988 Jean-Michel Basquiat dies

1995 eBay founded

1989 First electronic dance music festival Love Parade in Berlin

2018 Winter Olympic Games in Pyeongchang, South Korea

2011 After 14 years of collaboration, Dior suspends John Galliano

1985   1990   1995   2000   2005   2010   2015   2020   2025   2030   2035

GARETH PUGH

Gareth Pugh, whose collections are one part fashion and one part performance art, is one in a long line of British eccentric designers who imbue rebellion and the avant-garde into the fashion industry.

Pugh was born on August 31, 1981 in the post-industrial city of Sunderland, England. In his teens, he worked as a costume designer for the English National Youth Theatre and in 2003 he graduated with a degree in fashion design from Central Saint Martins. His graduate collection, which used balloons on the joints and limbs of models, attracted the attention of a fashion editor at *Dazed & Confused*, who featured one of his pieces on the magazine's cover. In 2005, Pugh was asked to participate in Fashion East's Fall 2005 group show at London Fashion Week. His success there prompted him to stage his first solo runway show for Fall 2006.

That first solo show, which featured a string of models in vinyl bodysuits and harlequin makeup, announced Pugh's arrival on the fashion scene. His playful debut—before the show began the designer tossed large black and white balloons into the crowds—was defiant in its anti-commercialism. Of the thirteen looks he showed that day in mid-February, there were few wearable or sellable pieces. The punk-infused outfits were complete with large ruffs, metallic checked coats, and patent-leather Doc Martens. Though at the time Pugh was squatting in abandoned buildings with little money to his name, the designer was not interested in sales, so much so that the runway pieces were unavailable for purchase. The same was true for his follow-up collection, for Spring 2007, which provided more wild theatrics. Inspired by Ridley Scott's 1985 fantasy movie *Legend*, "where Princess Lili dances in a white room and becomes her darker self," Pugh sent out a slew of faceless models wearing black-and-white checkerboard dresses, silver foil trench coats, and capes with 3-D shapes that doubled as wings. The looks, less clothing and more costume, were well-executed, providing the sensation, said Sarah Mower at *Style.com*, that "you're watching characters from some monstrous sci-fi computer animation coming to life before your eyes."

For Fall 2007, the theatrics remained, but the clothes themselves were more wearable avant-garde creations. "I was sick of people saying, 'It's crazy'," said Pugh of this collection. The makeup was dead-white and the hair was cut at all angles, but aside from a few see-through striped looks, there were gorgeously crafted coats—a black fur and patent stripe coat and an open black-and-white look among them.

For Spring 2009, Pugh made his debut in Paris. The show provided his signature sci-fi elements, as witnessed in the sharp shoulders and the angular limbs. The outfits, pure white on the front and all black on the back, suggested an emergence from light to dark, as well as creating an interesting visual effect. Pugh also played with historical references, incorporating elements of medieval armor, along with Elizabethan ruffs and Victorian underskirts.

When Pugh's Fall 2012 show opened with black paper rose petals falling from the ceiling, it was clear that a dramatic and moody collection was about to appear. The palette was primarily black and gray, with fringe, fur, leather, and snakeskin comprising his signature aesthetic. The angular lines, the animalistic, voluminous fur looks, and the molded minidresses all brought Gareth Pugh's dark fantasy to life. The show, many critics said, was Pugh's strongest to date, solidifying him as not only a master of theatrics, but also as a designer of clothes with more commercial appeal. Despite his addition of more wearable pieces, Pugh is consistently faithful to his roots, always staging spectacularly dark runway performances and pushing the boundaries of clothing-as-art.

1981 Born in Sunderland, Tyne and Wear, England
1995 Works in the costume department of the National Youth Theatre in London
2003 Receives a bachelor's degree in fashion design from Central Saint Martins; a design from his senior collection appears on the cover of *Dazed & Confused*
2004 Interns at Revillon; his designs are featured at a *Dazed & Confused* designer showcase
2005 First collection debuts under Fashion East umbrella; costumes Kylie Minogue for *Showgirl* tour
2006 Debuts at London Fashion Week
2007 Victoria and Albert Museum shows his work in its "Fashion in Motion" series
2008 Worn by Kylie Minogue and Beyoncé; introduces shoe line
2009 Debuts menswear in Paris
2010 Opens store in Hong Kong
2011 Guest designer at Pitti Immagine in Florence

Gareth Pugh, 2011

left
Gareth Pugh Spring/Summer
2009 show, Paris Fashion Week

right
Gareth Pugh Spring/Summer
2012 Prêt-à-Porter show, Paris
Fashion Week

1930   1935   1940   1945   1950   1955   1960   1965   1970   1975   1980

Rag & Bone Spring 2008 show,
Mercedes-Benz Fashion Week, New York

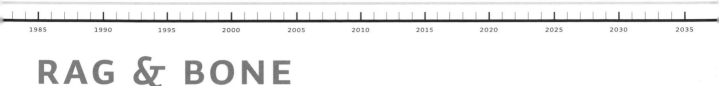

1989 The portable game console
Game Boy goes on sale

1998 Google is founded

2001 Wikipedia is launched

2008 Lady Gaga releases her debut
album *The Fame*

1985   1990   1995   2000   2005   2010   2015   2020   2025   2030   2035

RAG & BONE

The partnership behind Rag & Bone is a special one. Founded in 2002, the label is now designed and run by Marcus Wainwright and David Neville, best friends who first met as teenagers. To hear them speak of each other, it feels as though the company they've built, now sold worldwide, really is a labor of love.

They met in boarding school in Berkshire, England. Wainwright was two years older than Neville, so the two weren't close until they spent several months working together at a nightclub in Portugal. After school, Wainwright settled in London, but moved to New York after meeting his future wife during a stay in Mexico. The idea for Rag & Bone was born in New York in 2002, with the original intention of making a nice pair of dark denim jeans for himself. With that, he reached out to Neville, who immediately got on board to handle the business side of the new operation. Shortly thereafter, Neville joined Wainwright in New York and the two traveled to Kentucky, visiting factories and speaking with craftsmen; they spent time getting to know the patternmakers and craftspeople, believing that denim represented the history and authenticity of classic American workwear, a quality they wanted to reflect in Rag & Bone. Still, one decade later, the company produces many of their garments in these same US factories.

In Spring 2004, Rag & Bone launched their full menswear line and by fall of the following year they expanded the label to include a full women's collection as well. Their aesthetic is classic, yet modern, often influenced by British tailoring. Neither Wainwright nor Neville have any formal fashion training, but their goal from the beginning was simple: to make clothes that they and their friends would love to wear everyday. With that principle in mind each season, Rag & Bone strives for not only perfect fit, but also an aesthetic that blends the timeless and the modern, a look they achieve through a mix of both classic and innovative fabrics and consistently updated designs.

In 2010, the same year they opened their second store in New York, Wainwright and Neville were named Menswear Designers of the Year by the CFDA. They also staged an individual women's runway show for the first time, for their Fall 2010 collection. The show was a major success, filled with stylish separates inspired by the "crazy English guys

who climbed Mount Everest in the twenties in tweed." It was the epitome of downtown New York cool, with camouflage anoraks, fur-trimmed parkas, and striped sweater dresses. And then there were the accessories: stacked heels on hiking boots, long, textured scarves, and several knit bags and backpacks. Rag & Bone had introduced accessories for both men and women in 2007 and it was proving to be a very successful business for the duo.

For Fall 2012, their menswear was deeply rooted in English heritage, but they also incorporated the idea of frontier men, such as those depicted in *There Will Be Blood* and *True Grit*, men who do everything in their tailored clothes. With elements of workwear and traditional military details, plus some standout coats and jackets, the show looked completely contemporary. Their women's collection followed suit with a series of heavily layered looks. Blanket coats were layered over blazers and skirts, which were layered over pajama pants. Mixed prints, such as stripes and zigzags with polka dots and florals, added to the heavily styled look. Overall, the vibe was urban and cool, exactly what Rag & Bone does best.

Now in their mid-thirties, both Neville and Wainwright are married (Neville to celebrity makeup artist Gucci Westman) with children. So close are the partners that their sons were born within a week of each other. Of their closeness, said Neville, "Our lives resemble each other's very closely—we share the same schedule, the same family situation, we do the same things at the weekends. It's unusual to have a friend with whom you have almost every experience in common, so we can compare notes on it all. We're very lucky in that respect." The fashion world is lucky, as well, to have Rag & Bone's well-made classics with a twist.

2002 Rag & Bone founded by Marcus Wainwright and David Neville
2004 Full menswear line introduced
2005 Full womenswear line introduced; first runway show at New York Fashion Week
2006 Begin partnership with Bollman Hat Company
2007 Accessories for both men and women introduced; win Swarovski Award for Emerging Talent in Menswear
2008 Opens women's and men's stores in New York
2009 Open flagship store in New York's SoHo; introduce footwear
2010 Named Best Menswear Designers of the Year by CFDA; open boutiques in Nolita and the Upper West Side of Manhattan and in Tokyo

Marcus Wainwright and David Neville
of Rag & Bone, 2008

1943 First French "fashion week" is held

1955 Yves Saint Laurent begins as assistant to Christian Dior

1966 Michelangelo Antonio's *Blow-Up* is released in theaters

1975 Microsoft is founded in Albuquerque, New Mexico

1930   1935   1940   1945   1950   1955   1960   1965   1970   1975   1980

Rodarte Spring 2012 show,
Mercedes-Benz Fashion Week, New York

1983 Production of first commercial
mobile phone

1991 The World Wide Web
made publicly available

2001 First same-sex marriage
in the Netherlands

2018 Winter Olympic Games in
Pyeongchang, South Korea

980 Japanese retail company
Muji is founded

| | | | | | | | | |
| 1985 | 1990 | 1995 | 2000 | 2005 | 2010 | 2015 | 2020 | 2025 | 2030 | 2035 |

RODARTE

In the six years since its launch, Rodarte has rocketed to the forefront of the industry, with fashion's insiders swooning over the intellectual, meticulously crafted collections. Within this short span, the sibling designers have been showered with praise for their work on the runway, in magazines, and in film.

Designed by sisters Laura and Kate Mulleavy, Rodarte was founded in Los Angeles, showing first in New York in September 2005. Despite having no professional training—Kate studied art history and Laura majored in English literature—the designers are obsessive about their craft, employing couture techniques not often seen outside Paris ateliers. The sister's shared love of the arts has influenced several collections; references such as Japanese horror films or Van Gogh's *Starry Night* have figured prominently in designs, which often explore a dark, sophisticated form of beauty.

This impeccable workmanship combined with their dramatic personal touches have made Rodarte a favorite of celebrities, editors, and stylists, but the Mulleavy sisters, despite much media attention, have maintained their life in California, existing slightly outside of the trend-driven fashion industry. Their artistic and technically impressive creations are complex, not to mention expensive, to a degree that has forced critics to question their functionality. "We want to create collections that are beautiful," Laura said in a 2007 *W Magazine* article, "Wearability is subjective."

For their Spring 2012 collection, the Mulleavys drew inspiration from two past sources: the first, the fifties Disney classic *Sleeping Beauty*; and the second, the nineteenth-century paintings of Vincent Van Gogh. The nipped-waist dresses with swirling sunflowers, in vibrant yellow-golds, bright greens, and turquoises, seemed, quite literally, a world away from the prairie coats and apron skirts of the previous season's American Plains collection. Each season, it appears, brings a new theme. The Fall 2008 collection invoked not only a gothic darkness with its torn knits and blood red streaks, but also a delicate moment of full-skirted pastel confection clearly referencing Degas' ballerinas. They walked the line between darkness and beauty for Spring 2010 as well. Mixing futurism and the primitive, the designers combined plaid, leather, macramé, and

their exquisite knits along with lethal spiked shoes, black lips, and bare limbs decorated with graphic, tribal tattoos.

Kate and Laura Mulleavy, born a year and a half apart in 1979 and 1980, have that particular brand of familial closeness often found in twins—they grew up inseparable, both attended Berkeley, and now, years later, live and work together in Pasadena and Downtown L.A. Moving back in with their parents after school, they raised funds for their line by selling their record collection, using the money to purchase fabric for the ten pieces that comprised their first collection and coined the label Rodarte, their mother's maiden name. They took the pieces to New York during Fashion Week and made intricate paper dolls wearing the collection that they sent to various buyers and editors. *Women's Wear Daily* (WWD) took note and the sisters landed on the cover of the industry newspaper, leading to sales at Bergdorf Goodman and Barneys and piquing the interest of Anna Wintour.

Since then, their designs have graced the covers of *Vogue* and countless magazine spreads. Their intricate dresses are favored by some of Hollywood's most fashionable stars, including Cate Blanchett, Natalie Portman, Kirsten Dunst, and Elle Fanning. Their designs have landed on the big screen, as well, when they designed the ballet costumes for the Academy Award nominated *Black Swan* (2010). In addition to pieces at the Cooper-Hewitt, National Design Museum and the Los Angeles Museum of Contemporary Art, one exquisite off-white silk gown with chiffon ruffles and knotted silk rosettes is housed in the Metropolitan Museum of Art's famed Costume Collection. With collections for the Gap, Target, and Opening Ceremony, along with guest-editing roles at *A Magazine* and *Lula*, Rodarte's reach has extended into many spheres, proving that their talent and artistic vision will continue to inspire for collections to come.

1979 Kate Mulleavy born in Pasadena, California on February 11
1980 Laura Mulleavy born in Pasadena on August 31
2001 Both graduate with liberal arts degrees from the University of California, Berkeley
2005 Found Rodarte; first show
2007 Featured in the Metropolitan Museum of Art's Costume Institute exhibition *blog.mode: addressing fashion* exhibition
2008 Win CFDA Swarovski Award for Womenswear; win Swiss Textiles Award
2009 Win CFDA award for Womenswear Designer of the Year; collaboration with Target
2010 Design ballet costumes for *Black Swan*; first solo exhibition at the Cooper-Hewitt, National Design Museum

Kate Mulleavy and Laura Mulleavy of Rodarte, 2011

1967 David Hockney paints *A Bigger Splash*

1946 Founding of Estée Lauder
Companies in New York

1955 Mary Quant opens her first
shop in London

1974 Beverly Johnson appears
as the first black model
on the cover of American
Vogue

1930	1935	1940	1945	1950	1955	1960	1965	1970	1975	1980	

Jonathan Saunders Spring 2009 show,
Mercedes-Benz Fashion Week, New York

1997 Gianni Versace is shot
in Miami Beach

1994 First issue of *Vice* magazine
is published

2012 Olympic Games in London

2009 Barack Obama awarded
Nobel Peace Price

1981 First recognized
cases of AIDS

1985   1990   1995   2000   2005   2010   2015   2020   2025   2030   2035

JONATHAN SAUNDERS

Jonathan Saunders began his career in textile design, but soon the young Scottish designer was creating full ready-to-wear collections. His original prints and unexpected use of color come together to form a label that is as innovative as it is sophisticated.

Saunders was born in 1977, in a town called Rutherglen, just outside of Glasgow. His parents were Jehovah's Witnesses, his strict father a minister that frowned on materialistic things. Saunders began his studies by exploring furniture making, but soon his love of color and prints took him to the Glasgow School of Art and subsequently to Central Saint Martins in London. Within two days of presenting his graduate collection, which consisted of printed-chiffon caftans inspired by the album art from the Beatles' *Yellow Submarine*, Central Saint Martins alumni Alexander McQueen commissioned Saunders to create a bird-of-paradise print for Spring 2003. The colorful print found its way onto McQueen's floaty dresses, chiffon pants, and layered skirts that were well-photographed in the season's fashion publications. Shortly thereafter, Chloé and Christian Lacroix contacted Saunders for prints. Lacroix, then the creative director of Pucci, had the young designer create completely original prints, the first time in history that the house used patterns from outside their extensive archive.

In 2003, three years after graduating, Saunders debuted his eponymous label at London Fashion Week and just a few months later one of his designs appeared on the cover of British *Vogue*. That collection, for Spring 2004, was inspired by the art of M. C. Escher and Italian Futurism, as well as the past decade's rave scene. The show was the perfect mix of tight, stretch pieces that referenced dance apparel and feminine, chiffon dresses. The rainbow of colors formed a sea of geometry on the twenty-nine men's and women's looks, garnering Saunders some well-deserved attention. His prints, of course, took center stage, and in 2003 he explained that making them was no easy task. "It's a couture level of printing," Saunders told Tim Blanks of *Vogue*.

As Saunders progressed, his aesthetic leaned towards beautifully colored dresses that often incorporated both hard and soft elements. With famous fans including Sienna Miller and Kylie Minogue, the designer has created more than a few red carpet-ready pieces. For Spring 2011, the Scottish designer was inspired by the picture-perfect subjects of mid-century photographer Erwin Blumenfeld and the feminine designs of Claire McCardell. The result brought to life the very definition of pretty, with red-lipped models dressed in pastel dresses. The sophisticated frocks had bands of color, with pops of brighter shades mixed in with the softer tones and graphic florals adding hits of punch. He followed up the next spring with a similarly saccharine palette of peach, turquoise, and lemon yellow on sundresses, full fifties-style skirts, and camisoles. For Spring 2012, his prints were comprised of baroque swirls used on fitted sweaters and pajama-style tops.

For Fall 2012, Saunders used deeper shades of brown, red, and emerald green, mixing them with pale blues and lilacs that carried over from the previous season. His high-necked dresses and buttoned-up blouses came in rich florals and a series of plaid looks featured collegiate black banding at the hems. Notably, Saunders experimented with texture, using embossing and embroidery to complement fitted, double-breasted coats and delicate cocktail dresses. Saunders' strategic use of color and his artful construction of clothing had clearly come together to form a truly sophisticated collection with subtle equestrian references and slightly subversive femininity.

The intense colors and complicated patterns found in Saunders' prints call to mind many influences from art, but the designer has said, "My work's not referential." The look is all his own, a winning combination of spectacular prints and impressive craftsmanship that have made Jonathan Saunders one of England's most accomplished designers.

1977 Born in Rutherglen, near Glasgow
1995–99 Bachelor's degree in printed textiles at Glasgow School of Art
2002 Graduates from Central Saint Martins with a master's in printed textiles; Alexander McQueen commissions him to create a print; wins Lancôme Color Design Award
2003 Designs prints for Chloé and Emilio Pucci; debuts his own line at London Fashion Week
2004 A Saunders dress appears on cover of British *Vogue*; he designs prints for Roland Mouret
2008 Shows at New York Fashion Week
2008–10 Creative director at Pollini
2010 Collaborates with Debenhams

Jonathan Saunders, 2011

Jonathan Saunders Fall/Winter
2005/06 collection, London Fashion
Week

1930   1935   1940   1945   1950   1955   1960   1965   1970   1975   1980

1995 Toy Story is the first wholly
computer-generated film

1988 Anna Wintour becomes editor-in-
chief of American Vogue

2000 Tate Modern Gallery
opens in London

2010 The Burj Khalifa in Dubai
is officially opened

2004 Founding of Facebook

| 1985 | 1990 | 1995 | 2000 | 2005 | 2010 | 2015 | 2020 | 2025 | 2030 | 2035 |

PETER SOM

Peter Som works in the long tradition of classic American designers. His look is self-described as "effortless elegance and refined sexiness," only fitting for a designer who worked with the likes of Michael Kors, Calvin Klein, and Bill Blass.

Som was born in 1970 in San Francisco, California to architect parents of Han Chinese ancestry. He studied fashion design at Parsons School of Design, following his undergraduate education at Connecticut College where he majored in art history. While at Parsons in New York, Som apprenticed with Michael Kors and Calvin Klein, two masters of American sportswear. After graduating in 1997, Som won a series of awards, including being named as the Rising Young Talent in the CFDA Scholarship Competition and receiving the Golden Thimble from Parsons. One year out of school, Som signed on as the assistant designer to Bill Blass, while also working for Emanuel Ungaro's bridge line, Emanuel. In his minimal spare time, Som began designing and putting together his own line, working on and showing the pieces out of his Greenwich Village apartment.

Som's eponymous line launched with a fifteen-piece collection for the fall of 1999, and it had, wrote *Vogue*, "a Grace Kelly feeling about it." By September of the following year, with his line already stocked at Henri Bendel, Peter Som made his New York Fashion Week debut at Bryant Park. His ladylike designs, with their youthful elegance, quickly became a favorite of the fashion set. His muse was clearly a confident and sophisticated woman, but not one without some eclectic charm. His Fall 2002 collection was described as "fiercely feminine," a dark palette of predominantly black and navy paired with sharp tailoring and some heavy hardware." There were softer moments, as well, which included draped slouchy pants and fluid skirts and dresses.

In 2007, following many critically acclaimed seasons, Peter Som was asked to return to Bill Blass, where he had started his career as an assistant. This time, however, Som returned to the sportswear house as the creative director, brought in to revamp the company with a vision that he termed "stream-lined romance." Unfortunately, the house's finances were dwindling and, after just a year, Som parted

ways with Bill Blass. Then, in 2009, Som's own financial backer pulled out, sparking concern that the label would fold. Som hung on, relying on slow and steady brand expansion, several new licensing deals, and a string of starlets who consistently wore his designs, including Maggie Gyllenhaal, Camilla Belle, and Scarlett Johansson.

But what a difference a year makes. By the next fall Som was back on top—fully financed and in high spirits as he showed his Spring 2010 collection. The colorful and eccentric twenty-eight looks were inspired by Jacques Henri Lartigue's famous photos of Deauville in the 1920s, as well as Hokusai's wood-cuts and classic cruisewear. Striped tweeds and printed jacquards were applied to classic uptown silhouettes, infusing the overall look with an eclectic and slightly madcap spirit. The chic pieces were heavy on details, such as a jeweled neckline or a shock of colorful tulle. The mixed patterns and fresh colors breathed new life into Som's label, reinstating him into the ranks of New York fashion's best.

And Peter Som's bright and colorful outlook didn't end there. For Spring 2012 his collection featured vivid, photorealistic flowers in electric, multicolored brights. The skirt suits and shift dresses came in fuchsias, blues, and oranges, and the swimsuits featured high waists and a retro feel. The quirky-chic spring show retained Som's ladylike feel, but infused it with a dose of sixties surfer-girl cool.

Youthful sophistication and all-American ease is what Peter Som does best. His joyful designs, with their mixed prints and bright colors, are the industry's reminder that fashion is fun and shouldn't be taken too seriously, while his plays on the uptown classics have kept consumers coming back for more.

1970 Born in San Francisco
1989–93 Studies art history at
Connecticut College
1997 Graduates from Parsons School
of Design
1998 Begins work at Emanuel Ungaro
and Bill Blass
1999 Shows debut collection of
own line
2000 Henri Bendel picks up his line;
New York Fashion Week debut
2001 Becomes a member of CFDA
2002 Nominated for CFDA Perry Ellis
Award for Emerging Talent
2007 Joins Creative Design Studio
2007–08 Creative director of womenswear at Bill Blass
2011 Collaborates with Sferra on a line
of luxury bedding
2009–12 Consults for Tommy Hilfiger

opposite page
A model prepares backstage before
the Peter Som Spring 2012 show,
Mercedes-Benz Fashion Week,
New York

above
Peter Som, 2011

1958 Fashion designer
Claire McCardell dies

1945 French designer Pierre Balmain
opens a house of couture in Paris

1963 Mary Quant breaks through with
the invention of the miniskirt

1975 British punk band the
Sex Pistols forms

1930   1935   1940   1945   1950   1955   1960   1965   1970   1975   1980

Still from "Vanitas" by Barnaby Roper,
presenting designs by Camilla Stærk, 2011

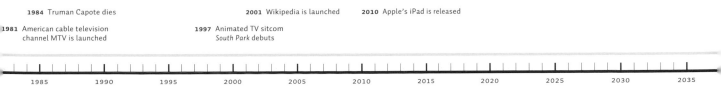
CAMILLA STÆRK

Born and raised on a farm in Denmark, Camilla Stærk's collections lean toward a darker palette, with fabrics such as leather and lace often playing an important role in her designs.

In 1996, Stærk moved to London where she studied at the Ravensbourne College of Design and Communication. Her graduate collection caught the eye of buyers at Browns Focus in London and Maria Luisa in Paris, prompting both to stock the young designer's pieces. Stærk's well-crafted early garments featured bespoke techniques and hand-sewing on draped silk tulle tops and leather skirts. After school, Stærk continued designing and her distinctly dark and romantic collections earned her reviews in several major magazines, including British *Vogue* who hailed her as "a future star." She also quickly developed a celebrity fan base, including Julianne Moore, Maggie Gyllenhaal, Liv Tyler, and model Helena Christensen, who not only wore Stærk's designs but also began carrying them at her West Village boutique in New York.

The Danish designer moved to New York in the fall of 2006 and immediately launched her current brand, Stærk. For Spring 2007, a collection she showed just one week after arriving stateside, Stærk staged her first ever runway show. The twelve pieces she showed at the Scandinavia House in New York were met with great reviews. For her New York debut, the designer diverged from her usual black and incorporated several pastels, such as pale mauve, dove gray, and dashes of turquoise. Several of the looks, including slim sweater dresses, were layered over latex tanks. "Even though I did latex in innocent and bright colors, there's something naughty about it," the designer said backstage at the show. The look was inspired by characters Laura Palmer and Donna Hayward from David Lynch's *Twin Peaks* series, a very American reference for the newly transplanted designer.

Camilla Stærk's inspiration is always a very real, very fundamental part of her collection. For her second New York show, for Fall 2007, Stærk's muse was the experimental fifties filmmaker Maya Deren. Deren's artful dressing during that conservative time in history served as inspiration, as did the "isolated romanticism" of Ian Curtis and Joy Division. For the following season, Stærk switched her focus to Woody Allen, crafting her twenty-one looks on his various lead actresses. She once again infused a collection of primarily white and black looks with pops of brighter color, adding checked cottons and a more casual tone to the overall feel.

For Fall 2008, Stærk turned her focus back to darkness and art, basing her Black Bride of the Moon collection on the Abstract Expressionist sculptures of Louise Nevelson. The polished collection featured knits for the first time, pieces toughened up with leather, and rubber. Her evening looks came in lace and coated silk, while her layered tank dresses were wrapped with belts of black leather fringe.

Camilla Stærk's personal favorite collection was for Spring 2012. The collection, titled Vanitas, was inspired by the late Danish artist Hans Henrik Lerfeldt. The luxe pieces were featured in a short film created by Stærk's husband, filmmaker Barnaby Roper. The dark fluid pieces were accented by leather, fur, and lace, giving the collection as a whole a gothic, romantic elegance. "There is a Danish sharpness and sensibility to my designs," she says. "The Scandinavian darkness myth is definitely true, and since I am drawn to that and it is part of who I am, it shines through in what I do," said Stærk of the collection and of her aesthetic in general. And with each season, Stærk's vision becomes more refined, incorporating inspiration from all sectors of fashion and the arts into her tough, yet elegant collections.

1974 Born in Denmark
1996 Moves to London to undertake a one-year course in fashion illustration at London College of Fashion
1997 Enrolls at Ravensbourne College of Design and Communication to study fashion with textiles
2000 Graduate show bought by Browns Focus and Maria Luisa; launches her own label
2006 Moves to New York City; launches new label, Stærk; her debut collection is hosted by Helena Christensen
2008 Opens boutique
2009 Stærk Signature launches

Camilla Stark

1942 Edward Hopper paints *Nighthawks*

1955 Yves Saint Laurent begins as an assistant to Christian Dior

1967 The musical *Hair* premieres off-Broadway in New York

1976 British band Joy Division forms

1977 New York nightclub Studio 54 opens

1930   1935   1940   1945   1950   1955   1960   1965   1970   1975   1980

Suno Fall 2011 presentation,
Mercedes-Benz Fashion Week, New York

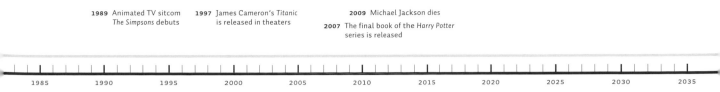

1989 Animated TV sitcom
The Simpsons debuts

1997 James Cameron's *Titanic*
is released in theaters

2009 Michael Jackson dies

2007 The final book of the *Harry Potter*
series is released

1985　1990　1995　2000　2005　2010　2015　2020　2025　2030　2035

SUNO

Within four years, Suno, the label created in 2008 by Max Osterweis, a filmmaker-turned-designer who lives in Brooklyn, New York, has set up thriving workshops in Kenya, been photographed for the biggest magazines, and graced the back of America's first lady, Michelle Obama.

The half German, half Korean designer was born in San Francisco and later attended film school at New York University. The birth of Suno, now known for its bold prints and traditional African textiles, is thanks in large part to Osterweis's mother, who, he said, "went on a safari and didn't come home." Instead she set up a retreat on Kenya's Lamu Island, a place Osterweis visited countless times in his twenties and early thirties.

It was during Osterweis's first trip to Kenya that he started collecting kangas, bolts of printed cloth traditionally used by Kenyan women to make clothes. He planned to make a few pieces for his girlfriend, an idea that never came to fruition, but he kept up the collection. The concept gelled in 2007, after the post-election violence in Kenya prompted Osterweis's concern for the country. He took a leap of faith and began designing, setting up two little workshops in Kenya and using his collected kangas as the basis for the brand. Shortly after founding his new business, Osterweis joined forces with Erin Beatty, a Colorado native who had held positions at the Gap and Generra. The aim of Suno was ambitious: to grow a profitable company employing local Kenyan artisans and ultimately affect positive social and economic change in the region.

Suno launched for the spring of 2009 a small collection that was produced almost entirely in Kenya. Made mostly from Osterweis's vintage fabrics, the collection was a hit, and quickly bought and stocked by notable retailers such as Ikram in Chicago and Opening Ceremony. By the winter of 2010, Osterweis and Beatty had generated enough buzz to stage a formal presentation at New York Fashion Week. The collection for Fall 2010 was confident and colorful, a print-on-print mix of fresh proportions and inventive styles. Oversized blazers topped printed pants and bright miniskirts were paired with cropped patterned jackets in teal, yellow, purple, and red. The overall look was youthful and exuberant, a true departure from Fashion Week's stereotypical self-seriousness.

The label quickly grew, with expanding workshops and employees in Kenya and orders at several major retailers worldwide. Then on the Fourth of July, 2010, Michelle Obama wore Suno at the White House. The lucky break, Osterweis said, was thanks to the line's supporter, Ikram, who had sold Obama several pieces of Suno that spring. The pressure was on for their Spring 2011 presentation, but the design duo met the high expectations head-on with another joyous, print-filled collection. Bold plaids and floral ikat prints found their way onto loose jumpsuits, collared shift dresses, and ruffle-trimmed swimsuits. Each pattern-heavy look was topped with an array of accessories, featuring strong collaborations with shoe label Loeffler Randall, milliner Albertus Swanepoel, and jeweler Lizzie Fortunato.

For Fall 2011, Suno stepped up the elegance, trading in the quirkiness for wallpaper-style prints and silhouettes inspired by older women. "It's an exploration of timelessness," said Beatty of that collection, which featured pops of color in an otherwise earthy palette. By the time Suno showed their Spring 2012 collection—their first runway show to date—the label had been nominated for a CFDA/Vogue Fashion Fund Award. Now carried at sixty retailers worldwide, the designers scaled back on mixing prints, focusing instead on more subtle patterns and a much more subdued palette of mostly black and white. Soft watercolor prints and wallpaper florals mixed with the occasional leather separate or pop of metallic.

What began as a well-intentioned response to struggles in Kenya has quickly become a successful business. Suno's charming, print-heavy designs have found a broad audience, positioning the label as a real player in the fashion industry.

1974 Max Osterweis born in San Francisco

2007 Following post-election violence in Kenya, begins designing pieces made from Kenyan cloth

2008 Founds Suno

2009 First collection stocked by Opening Ceremony and Chicago's Ikram

2010 First New York Fashion Week presentation; Michelle Obama wears Suno at the White House on the Fourth of July

2011 Collaborates with Loeffler Randall, Albertus Swanepoel, and Lizzie Fortunato

Erin Beatty and Max Osterweis of Suno, 2011

1949 Japanese clothing retail chain
Uniqlo is founded

1953 Decoding of the structure of
deoxyribonucleic acid (DNA)

1976 Founding of The
Body Shop

1979 Margaret
Thatcher
becomes
British prime
minister

1930   1935   1940   1945   1950   1955   1960   1965   1970   1975   1980

Temperley London Ophelia Bridal 2012 collection:
Elly Dress, Kelly Coat

1984 Prince releases his
album *Purple Rain*

1981 First issue of *i-D* magazine
is published

1999 Larry and Andy Wachowski's
The Matrix is released in theaters

2001 Jonathan Franzen publishes
his novel *The Corrections*

2016 Olympic Games in Rio de Janeiro

1985   1990   1995   2000   2005   2010   2015   2020   2025   2030   2035

ALICE TEMPERLEY

Temperley London is a mix of timeless femininity and English eccentricity. Designer Alice Temperley, who launched the collection in 2000, now produces thirteen collections a year, with pieces that exist outside of the current fashion trends, focusing instead on what women want to wear.

Alice Temperley was born in England in 1975. She studied first at Central Saint Martins College of Art and Design and then received her Masters degree at the Royal College of Art, where she specialized in fabric technology and print. Her launch collection of Temperley London showed in 2000 at London Fashion Week and was met with great reviews, prompting the designer to open a boutique in Notting Hill, London the following year. Her business grew and grew, mostly by word of mouth, and Temperley developed an impressive following of chic young socialites, models, and fashion editors in London. Her charming, ladylike pieces epitomized effortless feminine dressing.

For her Spring 2004 show, Temperley found her inspiration in a James Thurber story, "Many Moons," about a young princess who asked for the moon in order to recover from an illness. The fairy tale-like story resulted in a series of mainly pastel confections that included delicate lingerie-inspired camisoles and scallop-edged dresses. With lace trims, eyelet detailing, and plenty of chiffon, the collection confirmed Temperley's position as the go-to designer for gorgeous and breezy femininity.

For Fall 2009, Temperley presented her collection in New York, alongside a simultaneous video feed of the show so that editors and buyers in other countries could also view the line. The collection was inspired by the Silk Road, as well as Japanese origami, with folds on lapels and waistbands that referenced paper shapes. Expanding on her usual femininity, Temperley added sharp military tailoring and a voluminous cocoon-shaped jacket in a rose print, proving her range as a designer. In place of her of often youthful femininity, Temperley's Fall 2009 collection featured jeweled necklaces, ponyskin fez hats, and gold studs.

By the time Temperley London's Spring 2011 collection debuted, the designer had already added ALICE by Temperley, a more accessible contemporary line that focused on everyday pieces. The

Spring 2011 show marked the end of Alice Temperley's first decade in business and a steadily growing one at that. By this point, she was producing four annual collections for Temperley London, which included Spring, Fall, Resort, and Pre-Fall, as well as ALICE and a bridal collection, Temperley Bridal. For her spring collection, she revisited some of her classic looks, such as a delicate white sundress with a ruffled hem and feminine detailing. She also added a new toughness, accessorizing several of the runway looks with leather and chain harnesses and focusing on a harder edged look inspired by the legend of Guinevere and King Arthur.

Temperley's success is easily measured. Along with three stores in London, Los Angeles, and Dubai, the lines are also sold at countless retailers in over thirty-five countries worldwide. Beloved by a wide range of celebrities including Demi Moore, Reese Witherspoon, Emma Watson, and Rihanna, Temperley has become one of Britain's leading luxury brands. She has also found fans in the royal family, with both Middleton sisters spotted wearing Temperley's pieces. Pippa Middleton, the Duchess of Cambridge's sister, wore an emerald green Temperley London gown to the dinner and dancing party at Buckingham Palace on the evening of the royal wedding. The open-backed gown was a fitting choice for Pippa, who served as the Maid of Honor in the royal wedding, especially since Alice Temperley was named a Member of the Order of the British Empire for her services to the British fashion industry in March 2011.

With plans to expand her brand into homewear, menswear, and childrenswear, Alice Temperley has her sights set on creating a fashion and lifestyle empire. And, with all that she's achieved over the past decade, there's no reason to assume she won't do exactly that.

1975 Born in Somerset, England on July 22
2000 Founds Temperley brand; shows collection at London Fashion Week
2001 Opens Temperley London boutique in Notting Hill
2003 Opens boutique in New York
2005 Begins showing in New York; opens boutique in L.A.
2007 Opens a bridal boutique next door to flagship store in London
2008 Shows in London; opens boutique in Dubai
2009–11 Presents collections via multimedia installations
2010 Launches the sister brand ALICE by Temperley
2011 Shows in London; appointed Member of the Order of the British Empire for services to the fashion industry; designs Pippa Middleton's dress for the royal wedding reception

Alice Temperley, 2011

left
ALICE by Temperley London
Fall/Winter 2012/13 campaign

right
Temperley London Fall/Winter
2012/13 campaign

1930　　1935　　1940　　1945　　1950　　1955　　1960　　1965　　1970　　1975　　1980

Mary-Kate Olsen, Lauren Hutton, and
Ashley Olsen attend the 2012 CFDA
Fashion Awards at Alice Tully Hall,
New York

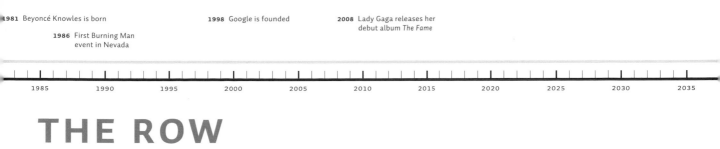
THE ROW

Celebrity designers are a dime a dozen, so when Mary-Kate and Ashley Olsen, the child stars who made their name as the youngest siblings in nineties sitcom Full House, *announced the launch of their luxury brand in 2007 there was much speculation.*

Just as quickly as the pint-sized celebrities became designers, however, the fashion world changed its tune. Before launching The Row, the Olsen twins had ventured into the world of design, but their mass-market collections had been sold primarily at large retailers such as Wal-Mart. The twins, who were born on June 13, 1986, in Sherman Oaks, California, were just barely of legal drinking age when they showed their first collection for The Row. By that point, however, they were style icons themselves, dressing less as typical twentysomething starlets and more with an eye to proportion and silhouette, mixing an impressive assortment of designer pieces with vintage finds.

The creation of The Row very much involved both siblings, but it was, according to the Olsens, Ashley's baby. Ashley left NYU before completing her degree in architecture and psychology because she, according to a 2007 *New York Magazine* article, wanted to make the perfect T-shirt. She approached her childhood friend, designer Danielle Sherman, and began to design a line of minimal, knit T-shirts in a neutral palette of black, white, gray, and beige. In addition to the tees, which boasted French seams and a hefty price tag, they also designed a small run of separates, which included blazers and miniskirts.

For their first runway show in February 2010, three years after The Row launched, the Olsens remained true to their early aesthetic. The vibe was all minimal luxury, with simple, chic pieces crafted from subtly opulent fabrics. "We wanted to do something low-key and straight to the point," said the designers of their nineteen-piece collection. Designed entirely in black, white, and navy, the simple palette let the understated silhouettes shine, like a pure-white corseted peplum top paired with wide-leg trousers or a black collarless wrap coat worn with slim pants and ribbon flats. The look was, in a sense, the opposite of the Olsen's well-documented personal style of oversized layers, heavy jewelry, and chunky boots. With The Row, the

twentysomething celebrities had successfully managed to design a truly sophisticated, grown-up line.

The subtle sophistication continued through the seasons, landing The Row in around 150 stores worldwide by 2011. By the time the Olsens showed their collection for Spring 2012, they had also launched a successful line of handbags, which, in keeping with the brand, consisted of updated classics crafted from luxury materials like crocodile and python, retailing between $2,000 and $20,000. But the bags sold, as did the expensive ready-to-wear, proving that the Olsen sisters had found their niche in the market.

The Spring 2012 collection was light and airy, with a soft palette of white, mint, and light pink on long, tunic-style tops and draped, loose-fitting pants. Of the collection, Mary-Kate said, "we wanted everything to float and breathe, or make a sound even." The light, elegant pieces were mixed with some show-stopping evening looks, including a silver and white caftan beaded with crystals.

The elegance, luxury, and simplicity that have become The Row's signature look was firmly in place for Fall 2012, where they used cashmere, alligator, and mink on coats and sweaters. Fashion critics have used many adjectives when describing the line, "serene," "timeless," "chic," "elegant," and "refined" among them. While in the eyes of some, they still may still be America's favorite twin child stars, Mary-Kate and Ashley Olsen have proven themselves as truly talented designers.

1986 Mary-Kate and Ashley Olsen born in Sherman Oaks, California on June 13
2005 Ashley drops out of NYU to design T-shirts with Danielle Sherman
2007 Together they launch the Elizabeth & James collection; launch their luxury brand The Row
2009 Inducted into the Council of Fashion Designers of America (CFDA)
2010 First runway show at New York Fashion Week
2011 Line sold in 150 stores worldwide; collaboration with TOMS Shoes
2012 Launch handbag line; win Womenswear Designer of the Year award at CFDA Awards

Mary-Kate Olsen and Ashley Olsen of The Row, 2011

1947 Founding of Emilio Pucci S.r.l. in Florence

1955 James Dean dies

1965 Luciano Benetton forms the Benetton company

1975 Microsoft is founded in Albuquerque, New Mexico

| 1930 | 1935 | 1940 | 1945 | 1950 | 1955 | 1960 | 1965 | 1970 | 1975 | 1980 |

Olivier Theyskens for Nina Ricci Spring/ Summer 2008 Prêt-à-Porter show, Paris

1988 The exhibition *Freeze* in London leads to the breakthrough of the Young British Artists

2003 MySpace is founded

1981 American hip-hop group Run–D.M.C. forms

1991 US band Nirvana releases the album *Nevermind*

2004 Founding of Facebook

1985   1990   1995   2000   2005   2010   2015   2020   2025   2030   2035

OLIVIER THEYSKENS

The road hasn't always been smooth, but Olivier Theyskens has managed to come out on top. The young designer, born in Brussels in January 1977, began his career at the age of twenty, and now, just fifteen years later, serves as the artistic director of the Theory brand, Theyskens' Theory.

In 2010, Andrew Rosen, the founder and CEO of Theory, tapped Theyskens to design a capsule collection for Spring 2011. The first collection of Theyskens' Theory was an instant success, with sharply tailored jackets that retailed for a fraction of designer prices, and several styles of denim. The commercial victory solidified Olivier Theyskens' prestige in the design world and positioned him as a major player in New York fashion.

Theyskens, who dropped out of the prestigious École Nationale Supérieure des Arts Visuels de La Cambre after two years of studying fashion design, launched an eponymous line at just twenty years old. The label, a strong, dark collection, did not have the financing to sustain itself, but it did gain Theyskens recognition in the late nineties as an up-and-coming avant-garde designer. In 2002, the young designer was named artistic director at Rochas, a French house founded in 1925. The old house, in need of a revamp, found just that in Theyskens, whose first collection for Fall 2003 was met with rave reviews. He quickly developed a famous fan base with actresses such as Nicole Kidman, Sarah Jessica Parker, and Jennifer Aniston, and, in 2006, the Council of Fashions Designers of America (CFDA) honored him with the International Award. His incredible gowns, which created a new silhouette for Rochas, were beautifully made and extremely expensive, often costing as much as $20,000. Unfortunately for Theyskens, the made-to-measure pieces were not able to be mass-produced and the house didn't have a strong accessories business to rely upon for revenue. The brilliant designer, also known for his anti-capitalist leanings and his unwillingness to support advertising initiatives, did not, it seemed, have the business savvy needed to survive in the fashion game. In 2006, the same year that Theyskens was recognized by the CFDA, Proctor and Gamble, the owner of Rochas, closed the fashion division, leaving Olivier Theyskens without a job.

His unemployment was brief, however, and within just a few months Theyskens was hired as the artistic director at Nina Ricci, a house that was founded in 1932. Since the fifties, when founder Maria "Nina" Ricci stepped down, the house had seen a string of head designers. Theyskens' first collection debuted in March 2007; ethereal and feminine pieces combined with fierce tailoring and shades of gray ranging from pearl to charcoal. With Nina Ricci, Theyskens maintained the house's signature femininity while introducing a younger style of casual, cool dressing.

Theyskens' last collection (Fall 2009) for Nina Ricci showed a distinct shift from the cool femininity of his first. Strong shoulders, chic leather jackets, and cascading evening dresses all sat atop stilt-like, heel-less platform boots. Before his final show began, Theyskens knew it was his last—he had already been replaced by the British designer Peter Copping. Not all was lost, however, for during his two years at Nina Ricci Theyskens developed a definitive style—a mix of poetic romance and youthful cool. His signature jackets and inventive cutaway skirts were praised by the fashion world.

His history had proven that while Theyskens was beloved by the editors, his designs were not often the most sellable, placing the young designer at odds with owners and businessmen. That is, however, until he met Andrew Rosen. Rosen, a fashion heir, founded Theory in the nineties and now operates as a major force in the industry, investing in several fashion labels and startups. With the creation of his line for Theory, Olivier Theyskens was able to see his designs produced at great volume, accessible to a much wider customer base. His cool, urban pieces, never short on imaginative tailoring or details, are finally available to the world at large, but not at the expense of his industry cred. If Olivier Theyskens has proved one thing, it is that in fashion, art and commerce can be brilliantly united.

1977 Born in Brussels on January 4
1995–96 Studies fashion design at the École Nationale Supérieure des Arts Visuels de La Cambre
1997 Shows first collection in Paris
1998 Madonna wears a Theyskens dress to the Academy Awards
2002–06 Creative director at Rochas
2006 Receives CFDA International Award
2006–09 Creative director at Nina Ricci
2010 Appointed artistic director of Theory and head designer for Theyskens' Theory
2011 Inducted into the Council of Fashion Designers of America (CFDA)

Oliver Theyskens, 2011

Riccardo Tisci for Givenchy Spring/
Summer 2008 Haute Couture show, Paris

RICCARDO TISCI

Religion and fashion may seem an unlikely duo, yet ever since Riccardo Tisci took the reigns at Givenchy in 2005, the two have been inextricably linked. Tisci puts it best when he says it is "dynamism and romance" that he brings to the brand, infusing and reviving the Parisian house with a dark femininity.

Having served as the creative director since 2005, Riccardo Tisci has infused the house with new life, one deeply inspired by the designer's own religious beliefs and emotions. The house was founded in 1952 by Hubert de Givenchy, known for his modern and ladylike designs that attracted several famous fans including Audrey Hepburn. When de Givenchy retired in 1995, he was succeeded by a string of short-lived designers: John Galliano, Alexander McQueen, and Julien Macdonald.

During those ten tumultuous years at Givenchy (1995–2005), a young Riccardo Tisci was learning his trade. Tisci attended the Central Saint Martins College of Art and Design, and after graduating worked for Puma, Coccapani (a Ferrari-owned label), and Ruffo Research, where he helped launched the careers of several designers. Then, in 2004, Tisci left to work on his own eponymous collection, which he showed during Milan Fashion week. When the offer came from Givenchy the following year, Tisci, planning to continue work on his own label, almost didn't accept. But as fate would have it, he received a call from his mother. "My mother called me and said to me, 'I think I am going to sell our house because your sisters are struggling … they need the money. I will go to a retirement home.'… And then I went to Paris, and they showed me a contract with all these zeros on it, and it was like help from God. I thought 'If I sign this, my mother will never have to worry again.'" And with that, Tisci signed the contract and became the creative director for Givenchy.

His debut collection, for Spring 2006, was met with mixed reviews. The presentation itself was far from typical: instead of a runway, the models circled slowly and posed in various areas around a stark white sphere. The clothes, which included sheer, feminine blouses and constricting pencil skirts, were mostly black and white, with hits of metallics and pastel nudes. There was no shortage of romance and elegance, but the feminine tone was balanced by a contemporary and slightly futuristic edge, as seen in the tough footwear—sandals with thick leather straps around the ankles—and the wide leather belts that covered half of the torso.

It wasn't until his Fall 2008 collection, however, that the rave reviews began to pour in. The romantic, goth aesthetic that Tisci had been slowly cultivating came together. Cropped jackets and black leather pants were paired with crisp white cotton blouses and sheer chiffon tops. The show opened with several all-black looks, topped with heavy layers of gold chains dripping with crosses. A cross motif ran throughout the show, with lace renditions on tops and dresses, a not-so-subtle nod to Tisci's religious leanings.

The devout Roman Catholic was born in 1974 in Taranto, Italy. His father died shortly after he was born, leaving his mother alone with him and his eight older sisters. Tisci has said on many occasions that he loves "romanticism and sensuality, maybe because [he] come[s] from a family with eight sisters." The designer's Catholic beliefs are widely known in the fashion industry, and in 2011 he was asked to guest curate the "religion" issue of *Visionaire* with a press release that began, "If you don't believe that fashion is a religious sect unto itself—and a fast-growing one at that—well, maybe you should pray a little harder." Tisci convinced several of his fashion friends to contribute to the publication, which included images of Carine Roitfeld with lace covering her mouth alongside photos of the designer himself suckling at the breast of performance artist Marina Abramović. Also included were images of Givenchy muse Lea T, the transgender model who famously appeared in the house's Fall/Winter 2010/11 ad campaign. In 2011, Tisci was asked to design the album art for Kanye West and Jay-Z's collaborative album, *Watch the Throne*. From the haute couture runways in Paris to mainstream rap album covers, Tisci's influence is far-reaching, positioning the designer as an important force in the world of fashion and art.

1974 Born in Taranto, Puglia, Italy
1993 Takes a foundation course at London College of Fashion
1993–99 Studies at Central Saint Martins
2000 Works with Antonio Berardi and Stefano Guerriero in Milan
2002–05 Creative director at Coccapani
2004 Presents capsule line in Milan
2005 Appointed creative director of womenswear at Givenchy; shows own collection at Milan Fashion Week
2008 Appointed designer of menswear and accessories of men's division at Givenchy

Riccardo Tisci, 2012

left
Riccardo Tisci for Givenchy
Spring/Summer 2007
Haute Couture show, Paris

right
Riccardo Tisci for Givenchy
Spring/Summer 2007
Haute Couture show, Paris

1943 Premiere of *Casablanca*, directed by Michael Curtiz

1956 Elvis Presley releases "Heartbreak Hotel," his first big hit

1975 British punk band the Sex Pistols forms

1930   1935   1940   1945   1950   1955   1960   1965   1970   1975   1980

Karen Walker design presentation, Rosemount Sydney Fashion Festival 2010

1991 The World Wide Web made
publicly available

1988 Jean-Michel Basquiat dies   **2001** Wikipedia is launched   **2012** Whitney Houston dies

1997 Animated TV sitcom
South Park debuts

1985   1990   1995   2000   2005   2010   2015   2020   2025   2030   2035

KAREN WALKER

*One of New Zealand's most high-profile designers, Karen Walker is now internationally known and loved.
Her quirky, irreverent designs are at once masculine and feminine, tailored and casual, tough and sweet.*

Walker was born in New Zealand, where she currently resides, studying design there in the late eighties. She graduated in 1990 and famously started her line with the equivalent of just $80, money that she used to purchase fabric for a shirt. By 1995 she had opened two stores, and three years after that her designs were stocked at Barneys New York.

In 2006, after eight seasons of showing in London, Walker debuted her line stateside during New York Fashion Week. Her charming, offbeat separates and whimsical accessories were an instant hit. The first New York collection was inspired by Land Girls, a term for the women who took over farm work in England while the men were off fighting in World War II. Walker used the idea of menswear—baggy shorts, for instance—but applied her signature twist of sexy subversion to make the collection feel completely fresh. Her floral prints and neon parkas were effortlessly cool, putting Karen Walker on the map in America.

Each of Walker's collections boast original names, such as "Young, Willing and Eager," "Queenie Was a Dog," or "Living with Cannibals and Other Adventures." The titles, while certainly charming, often don't do justice to Walker's involved inspiration. For her Fall 2011 collection, she delved into the soul scene centered around Northern England in the mid-seventies. During this wave, young people would spend whole weekends at dance competitions, returning to their jobs in the mines or on the docks on Monday. Explaining how she used that moment in history for her collection, Walker said, "There was this very working-class thing, with dockworkers' coats and caps, and then the racerback singlets that were worn for the more athletic dancing. And then," she added, "there was the super-femininity of some of the women's looks. They'd turn themselves out in their Sunday best clothes, with these full skirts that really moved on the dance floor." Walker's updates included a wall-

paper floral print on blouses, skirts, and dresses, accented with black vinyl. There were sheer chiffon dresses that looked ultramodern in midnight blue and a print of souvenir patches, mimicking the ones collected by those in the Northern soul scene.

For her Fall 2012 collection, Walker's multipart inspiration came from three varying sources: Jules Verne's *Twenty Thousand Leagues Under the Sea*, bourgeois Victoriana, and the sixties style of pop icon Brian Jones. Her collection mixed elements of them all, combining ruffled collars and a gold wallpaper print with colorful paisleys and A-line dresses. The look was polished mod with just the perfect amount of color and quirk. Walker's signature navy was a constant thread throughout, a color that she refers to as her "fundamental neutral."

Karen Walker's confident, yet slightly madcap, mix-and-match style has earned her a loyal following. In recent years, her line of sunglasses, which often include colorful, oversized frames, have been spotted on Rihanna, Alexa Chung, and Drew Barrymore, to name a few. Her aesthetic lands somewhere in between polished and eclectic, always mixing the masculine with the feminine, for a fresh take on modern dressing. With four stores in New Zealand, one in Australia, and stockists on several continents, it is clear that Karen Walker is a talented designer with a vision that's truly her own.

1969 Born in New Zealand on
December 4
1988 Starts her label while in her first
year at design school in Auckland
1990 Graduates with a degree in
fashion design
1995 Opens two stand-alone stores
in New Zealand
1998 First show at Hong Kong Fashion
Week; line is picked up by
Barneys; Madonna wears Karen
Walker pants onstage at MTV
Awards
2000 First New Zealander to have a
solo show at NY Fashion Week
2006 Acclaimed presentation at
New York Fashion Week
2007 Prix de Marie Claire award for
best creative talent
2008 Launches diffusion line,
Hi There From Karen Walker
2011 Designs costumes for Royal
New Zealand Ballet's *Stravinsky
Selection*
2012 Hi There diffusion line sold in
Anthropologie

Karen Walker, 2012

1969 Woodstock Festival

1955 Yves Saint Laurent begins as
an assistant to Christian Dior

1971 British fashion company
Mulberry is founded

1945 French designer Pierre Balmain
opens a house of couture in Paris

1964 British fashion clothing retailer
Topshop is founded

1930   1935   1940   1945   1950   1955   1960   1965   1970   1975   1980

Alexander Wang Spring 2012 show,
Mercedes-Benz Fashion Week, New York

1984 Truman Capote dies

1982 Michael Jackson releases
his album *Thriller*

2008 Tom Ford directs the
film *A Single Man*

2010 Apple's iPad is released

1985   1990   1995   2000   2005   2010   2015   2020   2025   2030   2035

ALEXANDER WANG

Known as the creator of the quintessential uniform for the cool, downtown set, Alexander Wang has created a fashion empire based on his relaxed yet sexy women's clothes.

His rise to fame began at the tender age of twenty when he left school and began to produce a small unisex line, including one infamous cashmere sweater with a girl's face on the back. The prototype, made using reverse intarsia, was spotted on a *Vogue* editor by designer Diane von Furstenberg. The *grande dame* of New York fashion inquired who made the piece, thus leading her to Wang, a recent Parsons dropout who had interned for Marc Jacobs, *Teen Vogue*, *Vogue*, and Derek Lam in rapid succession.

Born in 1984, Wang had moved to New York from California at eighteen to study fashion design. Raised by his Taiwanese-American parents in San Francisco and Los Angeles, Wang attended boarding school and took summer courses in design at Central Saint Martins in London. One of three children in a close-knit family, as a child Wang would sketch shoes on napkins and at age fifteen he staged a full fashion show at his brother's wedding reception, featuring a series of thirty plus gowns that he draped and stitched himself. The familial closeness remained: his brother Dennis is his chief principal officer, and his sister Aimie serves as the CEO. His adolescence was also spent socializing, a trait he has become known for in the fashion world, cultivating friendships at school that include long-lasting relationships with Victoria and Vanessa Traina, Danielle Steele's highly photographed socialite daughters.

Wang, who grew up in the nineties when minimalism reigned in fashion, says that those references, Helmut Lang and Calvin Klein specifically, influenced his streamlined, urban sensibility. And the evidence is there. His sleek little black minidresses and his expertly cut classic tees sell out season after season, serving as the essentials for the new way of dressing. Just before his third runway show for Spring 2008, where he showed oversized blazers paired with slouchy cutoff denim shorts, model Iekeliene Stange arrived at the fitting and declared the looks to be "exactly what I want to wear." At twenty-three, the designer was not only selling his designs to some of the country's largest retailers, but he had figured out exactly what his target audience longed to stock in their closet.

By the time Wang's Spring 2009 collection showed, a mix of sporty sweatshirts in Miami-inspired pastels along with his signature night-out black dresses and tough leather pieces, the designer had already won the CFDA/Vogue Fashion Fund Award, added a shoe collection to his label, and launched a diffusion line of T-shirts called T by Alexander Wang. At twenty-four, Wang was a bona fide player in the New York fashion industry and a regular on the party scene, his runway show after-parties already legendary. And this one was no different, with a performance by rapper Foxy Brown and hours of dancing—Wang himself dancing more than anyone else. Wang's dance moves weren't reserved only for the club; after each show the designer runs and dances and bounces down the runway, taking his version of a bow.

Since 2009, Wang has evolved, exploring more sophisticated design and asking "What does growing up mean for our girl?" His Fall 2009 collection showed a new polish—fitted crocodile jackets and fur-sleeved trench coats—alongside his usual tough sexiness. He was back to his signature black, creating pieces to sell in volume as the country sank into recession. Three years later, with a flagship store in New York and plans to open seven more around the world by year's end, Wang has proved himself season after season. For Spring 2012 the designer pushed the concept of sportswear to the limit, showing a BMX and motocross-inspired collection, complete with mesh bombers and sheer jerseys printed with motifs based on stadium seating maps. With each season, Alexander Wang brings fresh ideas to his designs, but one thing is certain: he always knows exactly what the cool girls want to wear now.

1983 Born in San Francisco on December 26
1999 Stages his first fashion show at his brother's wedding
2002 Enrolls at Parsons School of Design and moves to New York
2002–05 Interns for Marc Jacobs, *Teen Vogue*, *Vogue*, and Derek Lam
2005 Launches his first line of unisex pieces
2007 Introduces his full collection of womenswear
2008 Wins the CFDA/Vogue Fashion Fund Award
2009 Debuts his lines of footwear, eyewear, and T by Alexander Wang
2011 Opens his flagship store in New York in February; wins the CFDA Accessory Designer of the Year award
2012 A flagship store, the designer's second, opens in Beijing

Alexander Wang, 2008

1946 French fashion designer Jeanne
Lanvin dies

1951 J. D. Salinger's *The Catcher in the Rye*
is published

1956–59 Guggenheim Museum
built in New York

1976 Helmut Newton publishes his first
photography book, *White Women*

1930   1935   1940   1945   1950   1955   1960   1965   1970   1975   1980

Timo Weiland Spring 2012 collection

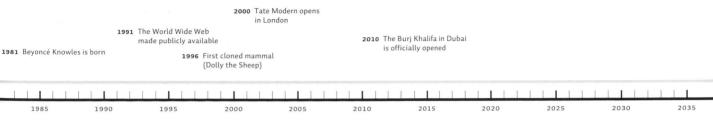

2000 Tate Modern opens
in London

1991 The World Wide Web
made publicly available

2010 The Burj Khalifa in Dubai
is officially opened

1981 Beyoncé Knowles is born

1996 First cloned mammal
(Dolly the Sheep)

| 1985 | 1990 | 1995 | 2000 | 2005 | 2010 | 2015 | 2020 | 2025 | 2030 | 2035 |

TIMO WEILAND

As the story goes, both Timo Weiland and Alan Eckstein were wearing formal ascots when they first met in New York. Their passion for formal, dapper dressing helped the two to discover an instant connection, prompting them to go into business together.

When they met, Weiland was working on running his small consulting business, while Eckstein had a business manufacturing clothing. Weiland had always had an interest in design, and by the fall of 2009 they had launched their unisex collection of neckwear, a fitting beginning for the pair of dapper gents. The pieces made waves after they were worn by lead characters on the hit television show *Gossip Girl*.

Weiland was born in rural Nebraska and raised between Florida and New York, moving to New York full time after graduating from Vanderbilt University. At an early age, his mother taught him to sew, but Weiland has no formal design training. Eckstein was born on Long Island, just outside of New York City. He attended the Fashion Institute of Technology, studying advertising and marketing communications and learning the business side of the fashion industry. When the word broke that Timo Weiland was slated to show a full range of ready-to-wear at New York Fashion Week for Spring 2010, the designer was just twenty-five years old.

The 2010 launch presentation, which featured clothing for both men and women, was a mix of classic preppy pieces with updated Edwardian touches. For Spring 2011, the pair were inspired by Bibi Andersson, the Swedish muse. They evoked the Swedish countryside with flared pants and tie-front blouses, as well as miniskirts, striped blazers, and patch-pocket jackets. The colors were bright and cheery, with corals, pale pinks, yellows, and reds. The menswear, which showed alongside the women's, was colorful and layered as well. A khaki coat with blue sleeves was shown over a striped shirt and graphically printed shorts. The models wore glasses in a nod to the designer's dapper roots, but there was an overall playfulness that came through in the patterned pants, cherry-red blazers, and striped socks.

For the following spring, Weiland and Eckstein staged a full runway show, inspired this season by a fictional journey. "It's Basquiat goes to Hawaii, goes surfing, and invites all his cool downtown city girls as guests," said Weiland. They used a mix of fabrics, such as brocade in bright colors like orange and magenta, as well as digital prints of florals on sheer chiffon. There were short skirts, like the cherry-colored dress that hit upwards of mid-thigh, but also long maxi dresses, such as the sheer green dress with an iridescent tropical print. The menswear remained colorful, too, with striped baseball jackets and floral shorts, as well as more toned-down pieces like an army green jacket and graphic colorblocked T-shirt.

For Fall 2012, they were inspired by the grunge era, designing velvet skirts and including more than a few plaid pieces. The reference was New York in the nineties when, said Weiland, "Artists were really able to be artists. We feel connected to that." While the womenswear instantly conjured images of a decade past, the menswear focused on more classic pieces and solids in subtle shades, such as camel, forest green, and chocolate brown. For this collection, the designers used fur for the first time, partnering with Saga to create removable fur pieces for coats and jackets.

Even with little formal fashion training, Timo Weiland has had much success in the industry. Their audience, as Weiland and Eckstein have put it, is "someone who appreciates the art of dressing." Combining their dapper sensibility with quirky twists and a colorful palette, Timo Weiland has created a brand for the effortlessly chic modern girl.

2001–06 Weiland majors in economics at Vanderbilt University

2003–08 Alan Eckstein studies advertising and marketing communications at the Fashion Institute of Technology (FIT)

2009 Weiland and Eckstein launch neckwear collection

2010 Expand line to clothing, including knitwear and accessories for both men and women; debut ready-to-wear collection at New York Fashion Week; collaborate with Bing Bang Jewelry, Albertus Swanepoel, and George Esquivel

2011 Inducted into the 2012–14 CFDA Fashion Incubator Program

Timo Weiland and Alan Eckstein

1930 1935 1940 1945 1950 1955 1960 1965 1970 1975 1980

Matthew Williamson Spring/Summer
2010 show, London Fashion Week

2001 Wikipedia is launched

1981 Ronald Reagan sworn in
as 40th US president

1999 Larry and Andy Wachowski's
The Matrix is released in theaters

2008 Lady Gaga releases her
debut album *The Fame*

1985   1990   1995   2000   2005   2010   2015   2020   2025   2030   2035

MATTHEW WILLIAMSON

Matthew Williamson was just twenty-six years old when he staged his debut at London Fashion Week and in less than two decades his colorful, expressive designs have become instantly recognizable.

The collection paved the way for the designer, who had previously worked at Marni and the British company Monsoon and Accessorize. Williamson was born on October 23, 1971 in Chorlton, Manchester, leaving at age seventeen to study at Central Saint Martins College in London. In 1997, three years after graduating with a BA in fashion design and printed textiles, Williamson founded his fashion house with CEO Joseph Velosa.

Matthew Williamson launched his eponymous line in September of 1997 with a collection he dubbed "Electric Angels." But, unlike most emerging designers, Williamson's list of models included supermodels Kate Moss and Helena Christensen, as well as socialite Jade Jagger. The collection featured bias-cut dresses as well as separates in vibrant shades of hot pink, magenta, and bright orange. The intricate, detailed pieces introduced Matthew Williamson to the London fashion scene, setting the tone of his signature aesthetic. The look, glamorous and attention grabbing, was an instant hit with the British social scene. For Spring 2000, Williamson showed a gypsy-inspired collection, with hand-painted dresses and sari tops. The magentas, purples, and reds of the spring line were embellished with fringe, sequins, and neon embroidery, giving the feeling of a well-heeled world traveler jet-setting in Ibiza or Bali.

By 2002, Williamson's bohemian prints and jeweled shift dresses were making waves on the small screen. His designs had been spotted by *Sex and the City* costume designer Patricia Fields, who dressed Sarah Jessica Parker, the show's star, in several of his dresses. Parker wasn't the only star wearing Matthew Williamson, however. Sienna Miller had become a friend and muse of the designer and Jade Jagger and Kate Moss were longtime fans. In 2005, Keira Knightly wore a purple Williamson dress to the London premiere of *Pride & Prejudice* and was quoted as saying "his dresses are like fairy tales." The same year, Williamson designed a green wedding dress for singer Kelis. The dress, with a classic bridal shape, featured a full skirt with varying shades of green, embroidery around the waist, and a lace-up, corset-inspired back. The designer, who has also been called the "connoisseur of clash" for his expressive use of prints and bright colors, often incorporates a signature peacock-feather pattern. In a 2009 interview, he explained that his "design philosophy is to make women feel like peacocks."

In September 2005, LVMH approached Williamson to become the creative director of Emilio Pucci, replacing Christian Lacroix. His first collection debuted the following winter to mixed reviews. The designer left Pucci in 2008 to focus on his own line, opening a flagship store in Manhattan the following year as well as introducing a line of accessories, including shoes, bags, jewelry, and eyewear, and debuting a capsule collection with H&M. By 2010, Williamson introduced a menswear line, telling British *Vogue*, "In menswear, there is a fine line between boring and 'costume,' and I want to hit that sweet spot." In addition to menswear, Williamson expanded his brand with a bridal line, a diffusion line, and a resort collection.

For Fall 2012, as Williamson celebrated his fifteenth anniversary, the collection featured a series of slightly futuristic, coolly colored cocktail dresses and evening gowns. His sequined shift dresses featured mosaic patterns of gray, turquoise, and dark blue with accents of neon yellow, while the evening pieces combined tighter prints with grand washes of color on floaty, floor-length skirts. Williamson's exuberance came through, as always. The vibrant dresses and brightly colored accessories that comprise Matthew Williamson's signature feel-good style successfully incorporate both a love of travel and the desire to make women look beautiful.

1971 Born in Chorlton, Manchester on October 23
1994 Graduates from Central Saint Martins with a BA in fashion design and printed textiles
1997 Launches his label with Joseph Velosa; Electric Angels collection debuts at London Fashion Week
2002 His line worn on *Sex and the City*; collaborates with Debenhams, Ballantyne, Tann-Rokka
2004 Named Designer of the Year by British *Elle*
2005 Designs Elis's wedding gown
2007 Design Museum of London holds the exhibition *Matthew Williamson — 10 Years in Fashion*
2005–08 Creative director of Emilio Pucci
2009 Opens flagship store in New York's Meatpacking District
2011 Launches diffusion line, MW

Matthew Williamson, 2010

Matthew Williamson Fall/Winter 2012/13 show,
London Fashion Week

PHOTO CREDITS

Cover, p. 131: Courtesy of Temperley London; pp. 6, 12, 66, 68, 69, 84, 87, 88, 91, 108, 114, 116, 146, 147, 150: Karl Prouse/Catwalking/Getty Images; pp. 10/11, 50, 51: Ruvan Wijesooriya, Shawn Brackbill, Courtesy of Mandy Coon; p. 13: Michael N. Todaro/Getty Images; p. 14: Bennett Raglin/WireImage; p. 15: Alli Harvey/FilmMagic; pp. 16, 19, 136, 138, 140, 141: Francois Guillot/AFP/Getty Images; p. 17: Larry Busacca/Getty Images; p. 18: AFP/AF/Getty Images; pp. 20, 24, 26, 27, 62: Chris Moore/Catwalking/Getty Images; pp. 21, 85: Jamie McCarthy/Getty Images; pp. 22, 23: Courtesy of Yigal Azrouël; p. 25: Rabbani and Solimene Photography/WireImage; p. 28: Amy Sussman/Getty Images; p. 29: Henry S. Dziekan III/WireImages; pp. 30, 86, 111: Peter Michael Dills/Getty Images; p. 31: Jordan Strauss/WireImage; pp. 32, 33: Andreas Ortner for mytheresa.com; Styling & Production by mytheresa.com; p. 34: Neilson Barnard/Getty Images;

p. 35: Courtesy of Chris Benz; p. 36: Joe Corrigan/Getty Images; pp. 37. 63: Brian Ach/Getty Images; p. 38: Victor Virgile/Gamma-Rapho via Getty Images; p. 39: Frederick M. Brown/Getty Images; pp. 40–41: Ian Gavan/Getty Images; pp. 42, 139: Kristy Sparow/Getty Images; p. 43: Richard Bord/Getty Images; p. 44: Pierre Verdy/AFP/Getty Images; p. 45, 67, 101: Nick Harvey/WireImage; pp. 46, 64, 76, 78, 90: Victor Virgile/Gamma-Rapho via Getty Images; p. 47: Michael Loccisano/Getty Images; pp. 48, 120: Biasion Studio/ireImage; p. 49: Lorenzo Santini/WireImage; pp. 52, 53, 54, 55: Courtesy of Creatures of the Wind; pp. 56, 57: Courtesy of Cushnie et Ochs; pp. 58, 59: Courtesy of Julien David; p. 60: George Pimentel/WireImage; p. 61: Gareth Cattermole/Getty Images for IMG; pp. 65, 107: Jemal Countess/Getty Images; pp. 70, 71, 72, 73: Courtesy of Mary Katrantzou; p. 74: Jamie McCarthy/WireImage for Jenni Kayne; p. 75: Astrid Stawiarz/Getty Images for Jenni

Kayne; p. 77: Shawn Ehlers/WireImage; p. 79: Shane Gritzinger/FilmMagic; p. 80: Benainous/Rossi/Gamma-Rapho via Getty Images; p. 81: Serge Benhamou/Gamma-Rapho via Getty Image; pp. 82–83: Alexander Klein/AFP/Getty Images; p. 89: Carl de Souza/AFP/Getty Images; pp. 92, 93, 95: Courtesy of Richard Nicoll; p. 94: Jermaine Francis/Courtesy of Richard Nicoll; pp. 96, 98–99: Courtesy of Darren Hall; p. 97: Janice Yim/Courtesy of Ohne Titel; pp. 100, 102, 103: Courtesy of Thakoon; p. 104: Arun Nevader/FilmMagic; pp. 105, 113: Andrew H. Walker/Getty Images; pp. 106, 112, 152/153: Leon Neal/AFP/Getty Images; p. 109: WireImage for Harrison & Shriftman; p. 110, 143: Slaven Vlasic/Getty Images; p. 115: Vittorio Zunino Celotto/Getty Images; pp. 117, 125: Astrid Stawiarz/WireImage; p. 118: Fernanda Calfat/Getty Images; p. 119: Donato Sardella/WireImage p. 121: Chris Jackson/Getty Images; pp.122–123: J. Quinton/

WireImage; p. 124: Wendell Teodoro/WireImage; pp. 128, 129: John W. Ferguson/Getty Images; p. 126: Barnaby Roper/Courtesy of Camilla Stærk; p. 127: Courtesy of Camilla Stærk; pp. 130, 132, 133: Matilda Temperley/Courtesy of Temperley London; p. 134: Kevin Mazur/WireImage; p. 135: Jeff Vespa/WireImage; p. 137: John Lamparski/WireImage; p. 142: Lucas Dawson/Getty Images; p. 144: Randy Brooke/WireImage; p. 145: Thomas Concordia/WireImage; pp. 148, 149: Courtesy of Timo Weiland; p. 151: Danny Martindale/Getty Images

SOURCES

Haider Ackermann (p. 13), quoted in Nicole Phelps, "Fall 2012 Ready-to-Wear: Haider Ackermann," Style.com, March 3, 2012; Steven Alan (p. 15), quoted in an interview with the author, and in Matthew Schneier, "Spring Ready-to-Wear: Steven Alan," Style.com, September 10, 2010; Joseph Altuzarra (p. 21), quoted in Nicole Phelps, "Fall 2011 Ready-to-Wear: Altuzarra," Style.com, February 12, 2011, and in Nicole Phelps, "Fall 2012 Ready-to-Wear: Altuzarra," Style.com, February 11, 2012; Yigal Azrouël (p. 23), quoted in Sarah Horne, "Shirt Chaser: Is Designer Yigal Azrouël Really a Casanova," New York Post, September 10, 2009, and in Sarah Leon, "Cut 25: Yigal Azrouël's New Store Opens in SoHo," Stylelist.com, February 3, 2012; Nicholas Ghesquière (p. 25), quoted in Helen Wigham, "Nicolas Ghesquière," British Vogue, March 17, 2011, in Armand Limnander, "Fall 2001 Ready-to-Wear: Balenciaga," Style.com, March 15, 2001, and in Sarah Mower, "Spring 2008 Ready-to-Wear: Balenciaga," Style.com, October 2, 2007; Scott Sternberg (p. 29), quoted in "Where Does Band of Outsider's Designer Go From Here?," Esquire, June/July 2011, available online in The Style Blog, Esquire, June 14, 2011; Victoria Beckham (p. 31), quoted in Nicole Phelps, "Spring 2009 Ready-to-Wear: Victoria Beckham," Style.com, September 8, 2008, and in Nicole Phelps, "Spring 2010 Ready-to-Wear: Victoria Beckham," Style.com,

September 13, 2009; Chris Benz (p. 35), quoted in Jane Keltner, "Chris Benz," TeenVogue.com, n.d., in Romney Leader, "Spring 2009 Ready-to-Wear: Chris Benz," Style.com, September 8, 2008, and in Bee-Shyuan Chang, "Spring 2012 Ready-to-Wear: Christ Benz," Style.com, September 12, 2011; Guillaume Henry and Natalie Massenet (p. 43), quoted in "Guillaume Henry," Vogue.co.uk, May 11, 2011, in Nicole Phelps, "Fall 2011 Ready-to-Wear: Carven," Style.com, March 2, 2011, and in Alice Pfeiffer, "Carven a New Path: Guillaume Henry," Interview, September 30, 2011; Phoebe Philo (p. 45), quoted in Alice Rawsthorn, "Phoebe Philo's Third Act," New York Times: T Magazine, February 25, 2010, in Sarah Mower, "Fall 2010 Ready-to-Wear: Celine," Style.com, March 7, 2010, and in Mark Holgate, "Indelible Ink," Vogue, July 2010; Richard Chai (p. 47), quoted in "Richard Chai," Vogue.com: Voguepedia, in Meenal Mistry, "Fall 2008 Ready-to-Wear: Richard Chai," Style.com, February 6, 2008, in Meenal Mistry, "Fall 2008 Ready-to-Wear: Richard Chai," Style.com, February 9, 2012, and in "The Design Dozen," Newsweek, May 23, 2005; Rachel Comey (p. 49), quoted in Laird Borrelli, "Spring 2004 Ready-to-Wear: Rachel Comey," Style.com, September 13, 2003, in "Rachel Comey: Misses' Dress," Vogue Patterns, and in Alison Baenen, "Spring 2012 Ready-to-Wear: Rachel Comey," Style.com,

September 7, 2011; Mandy Coon (p. 51), quoted in Steff Yotka, "How I'm Making It: Designer Mandy Coon," Fashionista, February 6, 2012; Creatures of the Wind (p. 53), quoted in Steff Yotka, "How I'm Making It: Shane Gabier and Christ Peters of Creatures of the Wind," Fashionista, February 24, 2011, in Nicole Phelps, "Fall 2011 Ready-to-Wear: Creatures of the Wind," Style.com, February 14, 2011, and in Chelsea Zalopany, "Dress Code: Creatures of the Wind," T Magazine: Women's Fashion (blog), New York Times, February 9, 2012; Cushnie et Ochs (p. 57), quoted in Davina Catt, "Cushnie et Ochs Isn't a Fan of Your Bedhead," The Cut (blog), New York Magazine, September 24, 2008, in Meenal Mistry, "Spring 2010 Ready-to-Wear: Cushnie et Ochs," Style.com, September 11, 2009, and in Meenal Mistry, "Fall 2011 Ready-to-Wear: Cushnie et Ochs," Style.com, February 24, 2011; Julien David (p. 59), quoted in an interview with the author, and in Meenal Mistry, "Fall 2011 Ready-to-Wear: Julien David," Style.com, March 8, 2011; Giles Deacon (p. 61), quoted in Rebecca Tay, "Designer Spotlight: Giles Deacon," Elle Canada, April 2012, and in Meenal Mistry, "Fall 2012 Ready-to-Wear: Giles," Style.com, February 20, 2012; Patrik Ervell (p. 63) quoted in Tim Blanks, "Spring 2007 Menswear: Patrik Ervell," Style.com, September 21, 2006, in Nancy MacDonell, "Now Online: Patrik Ervell," T Magazine (Blog), New York Times, April 20,

2010, and in Laird Borrelli-Persson, "The Nifty 50: Patrik Ervell, Designer," T Magazine (blog), New York Times, January 15, 2010; Prabal Gurung (p. 65), quoted in Meenal Mistry, "Fall 2009 Ready-to-Wear: Prabal Gurung," Style.com, February 12, 2009, and in Ella Alexander, "Fashion Royalty," British Vogue, March 10, 2011; Christopher Kane (p. 67), quoted in Kirstin Innes, "Christopher Kane: Sexy Boy," The List, no. 572 (March 27, 2007), in Sarah Mower, "Fall 2007 Ready-to-Wear: Christopher Kane," Style.com, February 13, 2007, in Sarah Mower, "Spring 2008 Ready-to-Wear: Christopher Kane," Style.com, September 17, 2007, and in Sarah Mower, "Fall 2009 Ready-to-Wear: Christopher Kane," Style.com, February 22, 2009; Mary Katrantzou (p. 71), quoted in Tim Blanks, "Spring 2011 Ready-to-Wear: Mary Katrantzou," Style.com, September 19, 2010, and in Tim Blanks, "Fall 2012 Ready-to-Wear: Mary Katrantzou," Style.com, February 21, 2012; Jenni Kayne (p. 75), quoted in nymag.com/fashion/fashionshows/designers/bios/jennikayne/, in Nicole Phelps, "Spring 2006 Ready-to-Wear: Jenni Kayne," Style.com, September 14, 2005, in Alison Baenen, "Spring 2012 Ready-to-Wear: Jenni Kayne," Style.com, September 7, 2011, in Alison Baenen, "Fall 2012 Ready-to-Wear: Jenni Kayne," Style.com, February 9, 2011, and from the Jenni Kayne website, http://www.jenni-kayne.com/content/c/store/more;

Derek Lam (p. 77), quoted in "Date with Destiny," *Vogue*, January 2010, in Nicole Phelps, "Spring 2008 Ready-to-Wear: Derek Lam," *Style.com*, September 9, 2007, in Nicole Phelps, "Spring 2012 Ready-to-Wear: Derek Lam," *Style.com*, September 11, 2011, and in Nicole Phelps, "Fall 2012 Ready-to-Wear: Derek Lam," *Style.com*, February 12, 2012; Phillip Lim (p. 79), quoted in Amy Larocca, "Mr. In-Between," *New York Magazine*, July 30, 2007, and in Meenal Mistry, "Spring 2010 Ready-to-Wear: 3.1 Phillip Lim," *Style.com*, September 16, 2009, Anna Wintour, quoted in Anna Wintour, "Letter from the Editor," *Vogue*, January 2008; quoted in "Phillip Lim," *Vogue.com: Voguepedia*; Isabel Marant (p. 81), quoted in Dominique Simonnet, "Un Bon Vêtement: Raconte une Histoire," *L'Express*, September 6, 2004; translated in "Isabel Marant," *Vogue.com: Voguepedia*; Marchesa (p. 85), quoted in Meenal Mistry, "Spring 2010 Ready-to-Wear: Marchesa," *Style.com*, September 16, 2009, and in "Marchesa," *Vogue: Voguepedia*, http://www.vogue.com/voguepedia/Marchesa; Erdem Moralioglu (p. 89), quoted in Sarah Mower, "Spring 2009 Ready-to-Wear: Erdem," *Style.com*, September 18, 2008, in Sarah Mower, "Spring 2010 Ready-to-Wear: Erdem," *Style.com*, September 22, 2009, and in Dolly Jones, "Erdem Moralioglu," *British Vogue.com*, May 11, 2001; Richard Nicoll (p. 93): Suzy Menkes quoted in Suzy Menkes, "London Flourishes as Talent Seedbed," *New York Times*, February 20, 2006, Richard Nicoll, quoted in Indigo Clarke, "Against All

Odds," *The Age*, December 14, 2007, in Tim Blanks, "Spring 2011 Ready-to-Wear: Cerruti, *Style.com*, October 1, 2010, in Tim Blanks, "Cerruti Resort 2011 Review," June 28, 2010, in Tim Blanks, "Fall 2012 Ready-to-Wear: Richard Nicoll, *Style.com*, February 19, 2012, and in "Pictures: London Fashion Week," *BBC News*, September 17, 2008; Ohne Titel (p. 97), quoted in Laird Borrelli-Persson, "Fall 2008 Ready-to-Wear: Ohne Titel," *Style.com*, February 3, 2008, in Colleen Nika, "Dark Horses: Ohne Titel," *Interview*, n.d., and in Meenal Mistry, "Fall 2011 Ready-to-Wear: Ohne Titel," *Style.com*, February 14, 2011; Thakoon Panichgul (p. 101), quoted in Laird Borrelli, "Spring 2005 Ready-to-Wear: Thakoon," *Style.com*, September 10, 2004, in Laird Borrelli, "Spring 2006 Ready-to-Wear: Thakoon," *Style.com*, September 14, 2005, and in Nicole Phelps, "Fall 2011 Ready-to-Wear: Thakoon," *Style.com*, February 13, 2011; Preen (p. 107), quoted in Ankita, "Interview with Justin Thornton and Thea Bregazzi," *Maison.boutique.com* (blog), December 21, 2011; Proenza Schouler (p. 109), quoted in "A Conversation with Jack & Lazaro by Ingrid Sischy," *A Magazine* [curated by Proenza Schouler], 2010, pp. 14–23, online at www.ablogcuratedby.com; Gareth Pugh (p. 113), quoted in Sarah Mower, "Spring 2007 Ready-to-Wear: Gareth Pugh," *Style.com*, September 19, 2006, and in Sarah Mower, "Fall 2007 Ready-to-Wear: Gareth Pugh," *Style.com*, February 15, 2007; Rag & Bone (p. 117), quoted in Nicole Phelps, "Fall 2010 Ready-to-Wear: Rag & Bone," *Style.com*, February

12, 2010, and Rhiannon Harries, "How We Met: Marcus Wainwright & David Neville," *The Independent*, March 15, 2009; Rodarte (p. 119), quoted in "Kate and Laura Mulleavy," *W Magazine*, October 2007; Jonathan Saunders (p. 121), quoted in Tim Blanks, "Vogue View: Special Talent Watch: Jonathan Saunders," *Vogue*, December 2003, and in Sarah Mower, "From London, With Love," *Vogue*, February 2008; Peter Som (p. 125), quoted in Katrina Szish, "Vogue's Index Scoop," *Vogue*, July 1999, in Laird Borrelli, "Fall 2002 Ready-To-Wear: Peter Som," *Style.com*, September 11, 2006, and in "Peter Som," *Vogue.com: Voguepedia*; Suno (p. 129), quoted in Sarah Haight, "Five Minutes with Max Osterweis," *W Magazine*, September 16, 2009, and in "Showing Today/Suno," *Milk Made.com*, February 12, 2011; Camilla Stærk (p. 127), quoted in Laird Borrelli, "Spring 2007 Ready-to-Wear: Stærk," *Style.com*, September 11, 2006, and in "Barnaby Roper: Vanitas," *Nowness.com*, July 13, 2011; The Row (p. 135), quoted in Amy Larocca, "Attack of the Fashion Gremlins," *New York Magazine*, August 19, 2007, in Nicole Phelps, "Fall 2010 Ready-to-Wear: The Row," *Style.com*, February 16, 2010, and in Nicole Phelps, "Spring 2012 Ready-to-Wear: The Row," *Style.com*, September 9, 2011; Riccardo Tisci (p. 139), quoted in Lindsey Anderson, "Riccardo Tisci nearly turned down his job at Givenchy," *Myfashionlife.com*, March 22, 2011, in Cathy Horyn, "The Q & A: Riccardo Tisci," *On the Runway* (blog), *New York Times*, February 28, 2007, in Charlotte Cowles, "Riccardo

Tisci's Visionaire Issue Costs $495," *The Cut* (blog), *New York Magazine*, May 2, 2011, and in Colleen Nika, "Givenchy's Riccardo Tisci Unveils Album Art for Jay-Z and Kanye West's Watch The Throne," Thread Count: At the Seam of Music and Fashion (blog), *Rolling Stone*, August 10, 2011; Karen Walker (p. 143), quoted in Maya Singer, "Fall 2011 Ready-to-Wear: Karen Walker," *Style.com*, February 15, 2011, and in Maya Singer, "Spring 2012 Ready-to-Wear: Karen Walker," *Style.com*, September 13, 2011; Alexander Wang (p. 145), quoted in Anamaria Wilson, "Alexander Wang: Fashion's Boy Wonder," *Harper's Bazaar*, August 11, 2011, in Meenal Mistry, "Spring 2008 Ready-to-Wear: Alexander Wang," *Style.com*, September 6, 2007, in Doria Santlofer, "Hooters T-Shirts for Everyone," *Look New York, New York Magazine*, November 24, 2008, and in Meenal Mistry, "Fall 2009 Ready-to-Wear: Alexander Wang," *Style.com*, February 14, 2009; Timo Weiland (p. 149), quoted in Bee-Shyuan Chang, "Spring 2012 Ready-to-Wear: Timo Weiland," *Style.com*, September 11, 2011, in Alison Baenen, "Fall 2012 Ready-to-Wear: Timo Weiland," *Style.com*, February 12, 2012, and in Jane Keltner, "Timo Weiland," *Teen Vogue.com*; Matthew Williamson (p. 151), quoted in "10 Key Moments: Matthew Williamson," *Instyle.com*, Ruth Altchek, "Shock of Color," *Domino*, September 2008, in Jane Keltner, "Wild Things," *Teen Vogue*, May 2009, and in Jessica Bumpus, "Williamson Expands", *British Vogue*, December 12, 2008.

INDEX